THE AGELESS WISDOM OF LIFE

THE AGELESS WISDOM OF LIFE

BY

CLARA M. CODD

1967

THE THEOSOPHICAL PUBLISHING HOUSE

ADYAR, MADRAS 20, INDIA

Sold by
The Theosophical Publishing House
Wheaton, Illinois

First Edition © 1956
Second Revised Edition 1957
Third Edition 1962
Fourth Edition 1967

Printed in India

At the Vasanta Press, The Theosophical Society,
Adyar, Madras 20

PREFACE

DURING a long life, continually moving, dwelling amongst many nations, in myriads of hospitable homes, I have had an unrivalled opportunity of observing human nature and learning of life. That first-hand experience was enormously clarified and explained by the deep wisdom and truth brought to us by Theosophy. Now, looking back over a long life, the great Principles and Laws of our divine and glorious existence stand out clearly. It took seventy-seven years of living to discover them, but ah! how worth while. May I never forget them in all future lives, though probably the fires of youth will obscure them at first.

That is one of the compensations of growing old, the wisdom that comes to one. When we are young, how we suffer, how we rush blindly into all sorts of mistaken action, and then pay for it with bitter pain. But when life is drawing to its close, peace comes and understanding and fulfilment.

What I have learnt of life let me try to tell you, my brother-men who read these words, and let me offer you at the same time my affectionate and enduring good wishes.

CONTENTS

CHAPTER I

"THIS KNOWLEDGE IS THE THING WHICH MATTERS"

A MASTER of the Wisdom once said to a young disciple:

> In all the world there are only two kinds of people—those who know, and those who do not know; and this knowledge is the thing which matters. What religion a man holds, to what race he belongs —these things are not important; the really important thing is this knowledge—the knowledge of God's plan for men. For God has a plan, and that plan is evolution. When once a man has seen that and really knows it, he cannot help working for it and making himself one with it, because it is so glorious, so beautiful. [1]

This true knowledge, which makes all the difference to life, contains the answers to certain questions man has been asking himself ever since he was capable of thought. To him they are the most important of all questions, to be answered if possible, for they form the basis for all security and direction in life and living. So paramount is the need for these answers that all religions have essayed to give them, and, to

[1] *At the Feet of the Master.*

a certain extent, so also do modern science and philosophy. But the most satisfying, complete and beautiful answers are those given by the ancient science, concerning man and his method of growth on this planet, called Theosophy.

The term "Theosophy" comes from two Greek words which denote divinity and knowledge or wisdom. Thus we may define it as the Divine Wisdom. That does not mean that every Theosophist really knows it. The majority of the members of the Theosophical Society have a nodding acquaintance with the bare outline of its great ideas, but an occultist, in the true and exalted meaning of the term, is truly one who "knows God", or the eternal Divine Essence of all things. H. P. Blavatsky, one of the Founders of the Theosophical Society, describes it thus:

> Theosophy, in its abstract meaning, is Divine Wisdom, or the aggregate of the knowledge and wisdom that underlies the Universe. . . . It has existed throughout the endless cycles of the past, so that it will ever exist throughout the infinitudes of the future, because Theosophy is synonymous with Everlasting Truth.

Occult Science may also be described as superpsychology, since it knows so infinitely much concerning the nature and constitution of man, his method of growth, and his inevitable future. Occult Science or Theosophy must not be confounded with what are called the occult arts, such as astrology, clairvoyance, the science of numbers, etc., etc. H. P. Blavatsky has defined this very clearly. She writes:

> Occultism is not magic, though magic is one of its tools. Occultism is not acquirement of powers, whether psychic or intellectual, though both are its servants. Neither is Occultism the pursuit of happiness, as man understands the word; for the first step is sacrifice, the second renunciation.

Then she tells us what it really is: "It is the Science of Life, the Art of Living."

The great science of life inevitably leads to the even greater art of living, living beautifully, scientifically, happily. Is it not worth while to know something, if only the merest outer fringe, of that Science of all sciences and that Art of all arts?

But, it may be asked, who knows it and where is it to be found? It has been garnered and handed down through the centuries by generations of great sages and seers, and is today made popularly available through the medium of the Theosophical Society and other bodies working along similar lines. William James, the psychologist, once said that all great thinkers presuppose that there must be, behind all forms of knowledge, a *Root Knowledge*. What could that possibly be but the great knowledge of life and all its vast potentialities and powers? Just as with every form of knowledge, for example, the science of mathematics, there are the children learning that two and two make four, and at the other end the great masters of the science, such as Albert Einstein, so we, most of us, are children in the great School of Life, learning by experience, and with much pain and trouble, the elementary laws of life and living, but there must be, somewhere, the great Masters of that wonderful science of ourselves. What They have given us through Their agents, as I shall endeavour to show, throws enormous light on the dark problems of life, and answers so beautifully all those questions which man has been asking since the beginning of time. Fundamentally, they are these: he wants to know who he really is, why he is here, where he comes from and where life is leading him, what happens to him after death, whether there is a goal to life and, if so, what it is, and what the laws are under which that goal may be swiftly and happily reached.

The answers to these primordial questions, which the ancient and eternal knowledge gives us, I will endeavour clearly to describe in the pages which follow. Mine will be the fault if the description is not clear and satisfying, for the Sacred Knowledge itself is veritably the food of our souls, the sustainer and comforter of wandering and bewildered man.

CHAPTER II

WHO ARE WE? THE BODY

"WHAT is man, that thou art mindful of him?" sang the psalmist. "What a piece of work is a man!" exclaimed the greatest poet in the world. So godlike in some ways, so animal in others, yet how few really understand him. Dr. Alexis Carrel points out in his famous book, *Man the Unknown*, how much we know about *things* and how little about *ourselves*. The modern science of psychology is still in its adolescent stages, but it is full of promise for the future, for, as H. G. Wells pointed out, we have practically reached the limits of material instruments of research, but are treading tentatively on the confines of the soul, the science of mind and heart. Sir Oliver Lodge once said that it would be the province of science in the future to explore the hidden recesses of man's Spirit, and to map out the hitherto unknown country on the other side of death.

But man is never unrelated to the universe, and there is no power of his consciousness which is not connected with some form of matter, visible or invisible. Thus, his actions express themselves through physical matter. He cannot "act" without displacing physical matter. But where do his thoughts and feelings express themselves, and where do they originate, since they are more truly him than his physical form?

We must realize that we "see" very little of the real man with our physical eyes. He is so much more than appears upon the physical plane. There are depths beyond depths in him which are only, if at all, dimly cognized and understood. The intuition of man, plus the teachings of the great religions, posit him as possessing or having a "soul". But what that soul is, and where it is, is only vaguely surmised.

The different factors in man's make-up can be classified according to the angle of vision. In the East, where the science of the soul is far older and more explicit than in the West, he is variously described as possessing, or expressing himself through, five or seven principles, sometimes called *koshas* or sheaths of consciousness. For practical purposes the Christian division of three—body, soul and Spirit—is the most helpful.

To begin with the body, do we know all there is to know about it? It is not ourselves. It is something we are temporarily using or wearing, like a suit of clothes. It is an instrument of experience and expression, but it also limits and confines us. The derivation of the word body comes from the Anglo-Saxon *bodig*, from which we also get the word *abode*, and it means the "dwelling-place". "Here have we no continuing city." It can be described by many similes. *Genesis* calls it the " coat of skin " which the Lord God made and gave to men. Arnold Bennett used to call it the " human machine " which we, the invisible engineer, drive. But, as it is a living thing, which has a dim elemental consciousness of its own apart from ours, the definition of St. Francis as " brother ass " is preferable, or, as called in *At the Feet of the Master*, " the horse upon which you ride ". Supposing we could go nowhere except on horseback, what care we would take of that horse, how we would learn to feed, exercise and groom him properly, and not over-work him, although this is almost impossible for many! That is how we should treat our body.

Another definition is to call it the piano which we, the musician, need to play upon. This answers a question often asked: can we think without brain-cells and feel without nerve-cells? Much better. We do not originate thought and feeling in our bodies but in our subtler psychic selves or soul. There it is a species of vibratory wave-length which communicates itself immediately to the brain-cells, becoming, in the process, damped down or transformed to a lower voltage. The piano has no music in it. It is only a thing of wood and iron and ivory. The music is in the performer, but he needs the instrument to show us in some measure the music that is in his soul. When our bodies " die ", *we* do not cease to think and feel. In fact we can think more swiftly and feel more vividly when we do not have to set in motion the heavier particles of a physical body.

Then why have we got a physical body? To bring us into touch with this order of experience we call " life ", although life in other conditions is more glowing and vivid than here. As our physical body grows, matures, and passes on to dissolution, all sorts of events and experiences come to us. They reach us through the sensory nerves. From them we form mental concepts, memories, ideals, images, understandings, which are literally the food of our soul's growth. Therefore life is a very valuable experience, little as we understand it. Without it, many lives of it, our souls would never grow and develop. That is what we came here for. And the sign-manual of a soul's growth is what is called character.

There is one thing we may not have noticed about our body, and indeed of all physical matter—it changes all the time, never remaining the same from one second to another. After some years, the change is clearly visible, but it is going on all the time. All forms on the physical plane are *phenomenal*, a Greek word which means an appearance only. Everything we see here is only what it " appears " to be at the moment. It is not the thing itself. Behind it is the *noumenon* or reality, invisible to physical eyes because the eyes are adapted to respond to only a certain limited range of wave-lengths.

We shall understand this better if we consider the constitution of physical matter of which our bodies are an indissoluble part. We can never take our bodies away from the physical plane. When we leave them the atoms and molecules which composed them fly apart and go to form part of other forms, animals, plants and men. It is a good thing to realize that our bodies are not so very separate from our surroundings. They are made of the same fundamental material as the trees and rocks and animals around us, and there is an invisible radiation and exchange going on between all forms in this world.

But why invisible? Because we do not yet "see" the whole of the physical world, not by a long way. Occultism teaches us that all forms of "matter" in the universe exist everywhere in seven degrees of density. Indeed seven and three seem to be the ruling numbers of the universe. We are familiar with three, perhaps four, states: solid, liquid, gaseous, and then the all-pervading ether, which science does not see but has discerned. Occult Science tells us that there is indeed an etheric state, and that *that* exists in four degrees. We cannot see it, but then do we see the gases? Yet we are told that before the evolution of men's bodies on this planet is completed, the ether will become visible in the air. That is already happening. The majority of people, if they look out into the air on a bright, sunny day, will see innumerable tiny sparklets of light, dancing here, there and everywhere. There is nothing the matter with one's eyes. We are seeing the first and most material state of the ether, and the dancing sparklets are vitality globules streaming from the sun. These are absorbed by the etheric counterpart of the physical spleen and circulated along the nerves over the whole body and its organs. The shining vitality absorbed, the colourless particles are thrown out through the pores of the skin.

This radiation of used particles can be fairly easily seen. It is most abundant through the eyes, the feet and the hands. Hold the hand against a dull black surface in a dim light, and it may be that a certain luminosity will be discerned round the fingers. Do not strain the eyes, but if it is really observed we shall notice that the radiation follows the impulse of the will, and can be made to extend its radiation further. Dr. Kilner discovered this etheric radiation, and that certain changes in it indicated diseased conditions in the body. He also invented coloured slides to enable a person not normally gifted with etheric vision to catch sight of this radiation.

This kind of physical clairvoyance is rather rare. Psychic clairvoyance is much commoner. But to anyone possessing it to a mature degree the denser states of physical matter become translucent. They can see into the earth for quite a distance, see through the walls of a house, through a closed box, see the organs working in a physical body, in fact they have what may be called X-ray eyes, responding to a far wider and deeper range of vibratory power than ordinarily. The writer has personally met two doctors and two nurses who had this power naturally. Its immense value to medicine can be easily imagined.

The above facts show us one thing: that we do not get vitality from food. From food, highly important as it is, we get a balance of chemical elements necessary for the body. The vitality which uses them is absorbed from the light and the air. The sun is truly the life-giver of his solar system. When the sun goes down enough vitality globules are left in the air to serve us until he rises again next morning. If he did not, we should soon all be dead!

When a person is full of vigorous health, " on the top of the world ", the etheric radiations are strong and upstanding. Such people are givers of physical life to others. A very devitalized person has radiations which droop, almost like wet grass. Such take vitality from others, because they need it. Old people sometimes take from the young.

The etheric matter in us is also the basis for physical mediumship. Normally, this finer state of physical matter does not leave its heavier counterpart during life. It forms the bridge between physical events and the intelligence. Hence, when it is temporarily driven out by an anaesthetic, unconsciousness supervenes, and the patient feels and knows nothing. It soon flows back but sometimes takes quite a time to settle in again, causing temporary loss of memory or powers of concentration.

Now a medium is a person whose etheric matter is very loosely organized, and is easily drawn from the body to form a basis for taps, table-lifting or materializations. This has been photographed by many people, notably M. Gustave Géley, and Baron Schrenck-Notzing. Too much cannot be drawn away or the medium would die. But it is a devitalizing process, thus disturbing the etheric matter in a man's body. Thus many mediums become ill and devitalized, and so take to alcohol or drugs to revive their failing strength. Even from those who are not natural mediums, a certain small proportion of etheric matter is drawn when attending a seance. Professor Crawford of Belfast estimated it as five per cent.

There is another wonderful thing about the physical body. Like all objects around us it is a store-house of symbology. There is not a single object on this earth that does not symbolize or depict some eternal truth.

Now what is a symbol? The word comes from two Greek words signifying " something put together out of more ", that is to say, it is a glyph or epiphany indicating a greater thing which cannot be expressed in words or even in idea. It is a finger-post, indicating where, if we have the intuition, we may discern the spiritual and eternal Reality it portrays. But if we take the finger-post for the reality, the symbol for the truth foreshadowed by it, we are lost. We become " cribbed, cabined and confined ". Theological dogmas are symbols thus materialized.

So the objects around us are epiphanies shadowing forth eternities. If we could read them, however dimly, we should begin to glimpse the glory and wonder of Life. The eternal hexagonal form of all snow-flakes, the geometrical beauty of many flowers and of crystals, remind us of the saying of Pythagoras, "God geometrizes." In ordered and beautiful tones God speaks in creation.

Then, too, in the so far invisible side of the physical plane, lives a lovely fairy life. Sometimes the simple sight of a child or a peasant catches glimpses of it, and the tradition arises of the "little people" and the "world of fairie". Not untruly did the ancient Greeks people the country-side with the Oreads and the Naiades, etc. Man is not the only order of life evolving on this planet.

But he, in his familiar physical body, is the product of vast periods of evolution, during which the organs of the senses by which he contacts life here came slowly into being. They evolved in response to an inward urge. In the words of an ancient Indian scripture:

> Man desired to see, therefore the eyes; he desired to hear, therefore the ears.

Slowly the five senses unfolded and created the organs for their expression. We have a common saying about being "frightened out of our seven senses". Before the evolution of men's bodies on this planet is complete, he *will* be in possession of seven senses. The sixth is very near the surface in numbers of people today. Its activity shows in the rapid increase of psychic sensitivity so prevalent nowadays. It has its appropriate organ of expression, which is also, from another point of view, a vestigial one, the pituitary body in the brain. Its future use will be to bring into the waking consciousness the phenomena of the psychic plane. Later on, the pineal gland, linked with the pituitary body, will bring the consciousness of the spiritual worlds into the waking awareness. But by then man will be standing on the threshold of being more than man. Gustave Géley describes evolution in just these terms—the gradual passing of the invisible into the visible.

What a wonderful thing indeed is man, even his " working-clothes " of the body, his " school-uniform "! The ancients said that man was a microcosm, a little universe, reproducing in limited and symbolic form all the powers and potencies of the Macrocosm, the Universe. If we could truly understand man we would understand the universe. But then that may be true of all creation. Did not the intuition of the poet cause Tennyson to write:

> Flower in the crannied wall,
> I pluck you out of the crannies.
> I hold you here, root and all, in my hand.
> Little flower—but *if* I could understand
> What you are, root and all, and all in all,
> I should know what God and man is.

Have we not as children often wondered *why* we had two eyes, two ears, five fingers, etc.? There is a reason why. For instance, our eyes are connected with our mind, so we use the same term for both. We " see " an object, and we " see " an idea. The body should not be despised, that wonderful, intricate, delicately adjusted " horse on which we ride ". Alas! how often do we ill-treat and abuse it!

As before stated, it has a dim, elemental consciousness of its own, apart from the superior consciousness dominating it. This has a wonderful instinct for self-preservation, and, if we let it, it will strive to the moment of death to set right what we have set wrong. This extraordinary power of the body is what Nature-cure has hit upon and explores. It can work best when we are temporarily away from it through the gateway of sleep. Hence the ensuing refreshment upon awakening. A Bavarian doctor works miracles of cures of hitherto intractable diseases by merely putting his patients to sleep for long periods. Best of all can our bodies do this during sleep before midnight. Hence the old saying about " early to bed and early to rise ".

What a wonderful world of beauty and interest lies in man's growing ability to explore himself and the world around him. How little he knows as yet, and how much more there is to learn! Man has within himself a power of magnification far outstripping any known microscope hitherto developed. He also has a power of exceeding any known telescope yet discovered. Does this sound like a fairy-tale? (Perhaps the ancient fairy-tales were glyphs hiding occult truths.)

Man must get into touch with Nature again, reverence her, listen to her; and then by degrees, she will unveil her secrets and all her hidden beauty. Only to spiritual sight will she do that fully. Says *The Voice of the*

Silence, an ancient Tibetan scripture, translated by H. P. Blavatsky:

> Help Nature and work on with her; and Nature will regard thee as one of her creators and make obeisance. And she will open wide before thee the portals of her secret chambers, lay bare before thy gaze the treasures hidden in the very depths of her pure, virgin bosom. Unsullied by the hand of matter, she shows her treasures only to the eye of Spirit—the eye which never closes, the eye for which there is no veil in all her kingdoms.

CHAPTER III

WHO ARE WE? THE SOUL

We speak of "having a soul" as if it were a possession belonging to us somewhere. Perhaps we picture it as floating above us, or dwelling inside us. I remember many years ago a young medical student telling me one day how he had spent the morning dissecting a man's brain, especially the curious little body called the pituitary body. "You know," he said to me, "no doctor really knows what it is used for.[1] But I have a great idea. I think it is where we keep our souls!" I suppose he thought his soul was about the size of a bee and issued from his mouth at death like the pictures of the Egyptian "Ka".

We can understand the soul better if we go to the derivation of the word. It is a translation in the New Testament of the Greek word *psyche*, which also gives us the words "psychical" and "psychological". Psychical research and psychology are modern attempts to explore the world of the soul. Psychical research explores it from the standpoint of matter or form, to find out what it is made of, what it looks like,

[1] They do now—C.M.C.

whether it can be photographed, etc. Psychology also attempts to explore the world of the soul, but from the standpoint of its powers of consciousness and how they work. The soul is the thinking, feeling self which goes on thinking and feeling even better and more vividly when separated from the instrument of the physical body.

But what does it look like? Where is it? Does it have a material form? These questions are answered for us by Occult Science. The soul-body is still material, has form and substance. But the matter of which it is composed is not physical, nor can it be seen by physical eyes or contacted by the physical senses.

Where is this other kind of matter and what is it like? The world of matter of which our soul-bodies are composed is not far away, beyond the stars, but here and now all round us, permeating and interpenetrating the whole physical world. Just as our physical bodies are for ever part of the physical world and can never be taken away from it, so our souls or psychic selves are part of the interpenetrating, surrounding psychic world, and they surround and interpenetrate the physical counterpart.

In order to understand this better, let us go back in thought to the constitution of the physical world. It has already been stated that all forms of matter exist in seven degrees of density. We know of solid, liquid, gaseous, and the all-pervading ethers, postulated but not seen by science. These states are all resolvable the one into the other. For instance, ice can be converted into water, and water into steam. What are the four states of ether like, especially the last? Let us call it the atomic state.

The final atoms of the physical plane are not lifeless things wedged together like the sections of a honeycomb. They are incredibly alive, whirling, flashing, singing vortices of force. They can be " seen " by that human power of magnification mentioned in the last chapter. Then it will be observed that they are whirling vortices of energy from another plane having three principal movements. They follow their own orbit, whirl round their own axis, and have besides a rhythmic in-and-out movement, almost like lungs breathing or hearts beating. There are two varieties. In one the inner energy whirls from the right to the left; in the other from the left to the right. We might almost call them male and female, or positive and negative vortices of force. The one kind attracts the other kind, so grouping themselves in miniature systems, like a microscopic solar system, they form the second sub-plane of the physical world. These aggregates attract other aggregates, thus forming the third and denser sub-plane, and so down to the chemical elements and the states well known to us.

But the question is, through what are the whirling vortices moving, since it is impossible for us to picture " nothing "? The answer is through the infinitely more subtle, the far more rapidly vibrating, matter of the surrounding psychic or astral world, which permeates and surrounds our known physical world far more perfectly than water permeates a sponge.

What is matter in that astral world like and who sees it? Certain states of it can be seen by developed psychic or clairvoyant vision. It seems to have certain laws of its own which are not quite like those which govern physical matter. For instance, in ever-increasing degree, as subtler and subtler states of psychic matter are reached, it is self-luminous, shining from within by its own inherent light. This lends it a sparkling appearance which caused the medieval alchemists when they saw it to name it "astral" or starry. It is a world without shadows, needing no luminary, such as the sun or the moon. It is also totally unaffected by heat or cold, neither expanding with the one nor contracting with the other. This means that when we are using our psychic vehicles of consciousness away from our bodies we are not conscious of either heat or cold.

Psychic matter is immensely susceptible to the vibratory wave-lengths of emotion and thought. There these forces are living, creative powers, fashioning our psychic selves and our psychic surroundings all the time. To a certain extent this can be seen translated into the physical self, as witness the lines and expression brought about in the physical face and the psychosomatic origin of many diseases.

Just as the psychic world interpenetrates and surrounds the physical world, so do our souls, or psychic selves, interpenetrate and surround our physical bodies, and being composed of a subtler, more volatile form of matter, radiate for quite a little distance all round us. This luminous radiation is sometimes caught sight of, and is technically called the "aura". Some sensitive people in the past must have caught sight of it, and so it is depicted round angels and saints and in the East round statues and pictures of the Lord Buddha.

The subtle body and radiation change from moment to moment, according to the passing thoughts, emotions and moods. Every type of emotion means a certain wave-length in this shining body and shows as living colour; not opaque, dead, flat colour, but living, vibrating, shining colour. These hues do not mix as paints do. Each of them being a definite vibratory rate, many different rates and hence many different hues can co-exist in one psychic body.

This is where we first think and feel and the subtle vibration is at once communicated to the accompanying brain and nerve-cells, causing in them a synchronous vibration, though considerably "damped down" since physical matter cannot vibrate as quickly as psychic matter, thus carrying through the thought and feeling to the physical consciousness.

Thought is a form-builder, emotion is a moving force. The very word "emotion" means the "moving force". Thought alone tends to become static, emotion in excess to become irregular and uncontrolled. Emotion colours life, gives it vitality, and in the psychic body it may be seen as glowing, scintillating waves of colour. These hues depict emotional changes, and their meaning has passed into many common sayings. We speak of a man's outlook being "coloured" by his prejudices and upbringing. It is a fact that none of us sees life as it is, but mostly through the coloured window of our own psychological condition. We see mostly what we look for; the world gives us mostly what we give to it.

The darker, heavier, more slowly vibrating conditions are depicted in our psychic bodies by the darker, more opaque shades. The higher and purer the emotion the more brilliant, the lovelier, is the colour. These more brilliant shades tend to colour the upper part of the psychic emanation, whilst those expressing less desirable feelings tend to colour the lower part. It has been suggested that the Christian custom of kneeling in prayer may have arisen from an unconscious desire to cut off that lower part.

All colours belonging to the rosy range of hues depict stages of love or passion, as also certain forms of anger and courage. Pure love shows as a wonderful rosy radiance. We often speak of persons as "seeing the world through rosy spectacles". This is true, through the rosy spectacles of a happy, loving self. This colour, even on the physical plane, tends to be cheering, as witness a rosy lamp-shade.

Selfish passion shows as a very unpleasant murky purple-red; anger as a flashing crimson, sometimes radiating darts towards the object of angry passion. Courage shows as a vivid scarlet, the "red badge of courage", also as a steady, strong and straight radiation of the whole psychic body.

Animals and plants also possess psychic counterparts with smaller radiations, and a slight pink haze can be detected rising from a happy, purring cat.

All shades of blue depict quieter, more peaceful, more religious emotions, from the dirty blue mixed with grey which an ignorant fetish-worshipper might exhibit, to the deep sapphire blue of pure-hearted devotion to a divine ideal, and the paler hue of devotion to a metaphysical ideal. Devotion to a religious ideal is often accompanied by prayer and aspiration. Prayer shows as an ascending spire of scintillating blue light, and is *always* answered by a rain of light and blessing whether felt by the physical consciousness or not. Aspiration generally takes the form of stars flying upwards. Hence the Lady Chapels in churches are often coloured blue, studded with stars, and the Lord's Mother is always depicted in a blue mantle, emblematic of the devotion which was supremely hers. Perhaps we may liken the spire of a church to a prayer in stone. Indigo blue indicates the action of higher, metaphysical thought. Blue on the physical plane is a "restful" colour.

Yellow depicts the play of the intellect, and generally shines round the head in the accompanying aura. This is the easiest colour to be discerned and a fair number of people detect it in preachers and speakers, for just then the intellect is very active. From the dull yellow of an inferior intellect to the glorious shining radiation of a spiritual man, it constitutes a " halo " which all men possess in some measure. It may be that simple peasantry or artists in earlier times saw this halo, and so saints and angels came to be drawn with shining halos. Orange denotes pride.

Green is a very adaptable colour, it harmonizes with all others, and it means a similar capacity in the aura. From the dirty grey-green of deceit—which means responding to others for one's own advantage—through the emerald green of an adaptable, " all things to all men " kind of nature, it rises to the lovely apple-green of divine sympathy, responding to others to *their* advantage. A dirty green flecked with irritated sparks of anger shows that the feeling of possessive jealousy is present. It sometimes takes the form of a permanent, curiously watching " thought-form "—the " green-eyed monster " so well known to all.

Violet also means many things. A very dark shade indicates a certain acquaintance with the darker forms of magic, whilst a lovely violet, which only appears in the higher reaches of the aura, means high spirituality and divine understanding.

White light indicates a consciousness of the divine " Will-to-good ", and shafts of white light mean that the person concerned is a channel for the Divine Light and Blessing.

Black, inky clouds indicate malice and ill-will. A mild form of this is called the " sulks "; also sometimes the " black dog " or a " chip " on the shoulder.

Grey indicates fear, depression, which is also indicated by a trembling and lack of stamina in the psychic radiations. When this is very pronounced, a state of panic supervenes where the person concerned has no more control over his actions. Greed and selfishness show as a kind of rusty brown. Both fear and greed can become so developed as to virtually imprison a man in his outlook, and can be carried on into the immediate states after death. The liberating forces are love and courage, for ever the saviours of men.

An occult scripture states that the disciple should surround himself in meditation with the "five sacred colours". It does not mean curtains in the physical world, but his shining aura should depict only these: the rose of love, the blue of devotion, the gold of enlightened intelligence, the green of sympathy, and the violet of spiritual intuition. Most people's auras are a mass of conflicting, petty emotions, which in the long run are devitalizing and fatiguing. The enlightened and controlled man radiates strongly a few big, generous, pure emotions. Therefore he is always a force for good, uplifting and comforting all he comes into contact with, and a man of calm and impressive presence.

For it must not be forgotten that emotions are "catching". The stronger tune up others; the weak tend to catch and reproduce the more depressive forces. Do we not all know of the "wet-blanket" whose appearance causes the spirits of an assembled company to run down to zero? And to whom do we turn in moments of distress and despair, but to those stronger, steadier, unselfish souls who are to others as shady trees in a barren land? Even in the soul-world, in the world of feeling and thought, no man liveth or dieth to himself alone. He inevitably affects others and is in turn affected by them.

It is interesting to note, as life follows life in the great School of Life, how gradually the auric colours clarify and enlarge. Vices and virtues are not different things. They are intimately related. There is an Indian simile of the growth of the soul as a lotus flower which has its roots in the mud of the tank or lake, grows up through the water, and at last in the sunshine and air the lovely flower unfolds and fills the air with its fragrance. Thus by slow evolution and experience the red of possessive passion becomes the rose of unselfish love; the grey-blue of ignorant, superstitious worship becomes the " heavenly blue " of true devotion, the grey-green of deceit grows into the apple-green of divine sympathy, the muddy yellow of the undeveloped intellect becomes the shining gold of the spiritual intelligence; the gloomy purple of earthly magic becomes the glowing lavender of awakened spirituality. As *The Voice of the Silence* says:

> Out of the furnace of man's life and its black smoke, winged flames arise, flames purified, that soaring onward, 'neath the Karmic eye, weave in the end the fabric glorified of the three vestures of the Path.

Thus, out of so-called " evil ", ultimately comes good.

CHAPTER IV

WHO ARE WE? THE SPIRIT

BUT even our soul, the changing, developing, psychological self, is not the Real Man. It is but a finer vesture of the Self. We can put it crudely like this. The spiritual Self in man is the real man, his soul-self is like his clothes, and his body like an overcoat for going out of doors. But who is the spiritual Self? What is he like? Here again let us go to the derivation of the word. Many people confuse the two terms, soul and Spirit, and think they are interchangeable terms. But in the Greek they are quite different words. Soul is *psyche*, and Spirit is *pneuma*, which means breath, life. God breathed into physical and psychological man the breath of life and he became a living, immortal Soul. For this is the only part of us that *is* truly immortal and undying and will live for ever, for it is Life and Eternity. It cannot be described, it can only be indicated by poetic simile and symbolism. Call it by whatever name we will; it is a spark of the eternal Life which informs the universe, a seed of Divinity holding in potentiality the powers and beauty of the source from which it came. It is a Word of God, spoken to express and yet to limit a Divine Thought.

If we call it a flame or spark, let us notice that however often we light a flame from a flame it is never diminished. Says an old Occult catechism:

> I sense one flame, O Gurudeva, and countless, undetached sparks shining therein.

For this is where the "angel in a man", as the Christ called it, has never left the bosom of the Father; the innocent One has never left the Garden of Eden, the Kingdom of Heaven within, deep, deep within. It is clothed with the garments of soul and body to gather the experiences of life. Sublimating those which can be the food of its pure life, it slowly returns after death to Itself, "bringing its sheaves with it".

But in itself, it is essentially pure and undefiled. St. Paul describes it thus:

> The hidden man of the heart, in that which is not corruptible.

He also describes it in other terms, as "the Christ in you, the hope of glory", and yearns over his converts until this Christ-nature "be formed in you" or brought to birth. The whole of the Pauline epistles are based on that truth—the essential Divinity of man. And that "Christ-consciousness" awakened, come to birth, in a man, so changes, so divinizes a man, that in the East he is called the "twice-born". Evidently our Lord had the same thought when He said to Nicodemus:

> Marvel not that I said unto thee, Ye must be born again . . . born of water and of the Spirit.

Fire and water, these two seeming incompatibles, have ever been the symbols of the divine and human in man, eternally struggling until the Divinity within has finally purified, redeemed, uplifted the soul and body, atoned for them with himself, thus making them the clear and flawless vehicles of the awakened and developed God within. This is the Adept, the Perfect Man, the Master of the Wisdom, the Christ or Anointed One of man's aspiring and God's intending for every one of us. There is no man, however ignorant and degraded, however evil, who has not somewhere this spark of Divinity; whilst he is a son of man he is also and for ever a Son of the Most High.

He is born of two forces: matter, Mother Earth, always symbolized in ancient scriptures as feminine, negative, naturally dropping downwards as a drop of water; and Spirit, an ever-mounting flame, soaring upwards. Even a planet, a solar system, is born of these two "poles of opposites", a fire-mist. We are always aware of the pull of these two forces in us, one leading us upward, one dragging us downward. St. Paul, again, speaks of it, calling himself a wretched man, who is drawn by each in turn and who sometimes succumbs to the lower. This is symbolized in the sign of the Theosophical Society, the interlaced triangles, one pointing upwards like a soaring flame, the other pointing downwards like water dropping.

The God in man is one day born (as the Saviour in the Christian story) of a human, visible Mother, our material selves, and a forever unseen, invisible Divine Father. As *Light on the Path* tells us:

> You will enter the light, but you will never touch the Flame.

From these two is one day born the divine, the Perfect Man. Meanwhile his embryo dreams, gestates, in the womb of human nature, awaiting the hour of his birth, when even then he has to grow to his stature and fullness. *This* is the unending glory, wisdom and bliss that man longs for all the time. Here are only "broken lights of Thee". Therefore, as H. P. Blavatsky says, let us await with patience the hour of "our real, our best birth".

Ah! what a long way to go for some of us yet! But it is helpful to be able in some measure to glimpse the goal of life. We are all travellers on a dark and stony road. If we do not know the goal, how long the way seems, how many times we stumble and bruise our feet! But if we only know a little of the glorious ending of the human way, the path is a little lightened, a little eased.

The Christ told us that the Kingdom of Heaven was *within* us, not outside us somewhere far away. All the great Teachers have told us the same truth. In another simile the Lord likened it to a "pearl of great price", for which a man would sell all he had to buy it. So shall we all one day strive to find it by "plunging into the mysterious and glorious depths of our own inmost being", but we shall only find it at the price of all that we have, for, in the great adventure of the Spirit, Heaven demands the allegiance of a *whole* heart.

But if we call it a " seed " the simile still holds good, for no seed can come to fulfilment unless it first of all " dies ". It dies in order to live and to reproduce all its hidden, in-folded potentialities and powers. Is it not one of the miracles of Nature that the tiny acorn holds within it the future giant of the forest? But first it must be buried deep in the ground, and no one may know it is there. So with many souls, no Divinity seems to be present in them. But, underneath, growth is going on. The first thing a seed does is to put down rootlets to give it strength to push up above the ground. Here is another miracle of Nature. How does a tiny, tender shoot push through the hard ground? Even when it finally appears only an experienced gardener can tell what it is going to be. " It is not yet made manifest," wrote St. John, " what we shall be."

But growth goes steadily on, and two forces from without aid that growth, sunshine and rain. The sun causes the plant to expand, reach up to the light and the air. The rain washes the plant, softens the hard earth round its root, nourishes it. So also grows the human soul and Spirit. The sunshine of human joy and success causes it to expand and reach upward. The rain of human tears should soften the hard earth, purify the soul, teach sympathy and understanding. Alas! it does not always do that, but it is *meant* to do so. H. P. Blavatsky calls pain the teacher, the awakener of consciousness. She also says:

> As soon as he begins to understand what a friend and teacher pain can be, the Theosophist stands appalled before the mysterious problem of human life, and though he may long to do good works, equally he dreads to do them wrongly, until he has himself acquired greater power and knowledge.

So by the alternations of sorrow and joy, and all the "pairs of opposites" in life, does man finally come to Divine Self-Consciousness, and to the conquest of ignorance and pain.

Finally, that towards which all antecedent growth tended, the flower, is born, and all the air is filled with its fragrance. So does the "odour of sanctity", the fragrance of spiritual wholeness or holiness, fill the surroundings of the truly awakened, developed man; he has become a perennial, unseen blessing to all that lives.

The humanity in each of us is the matrix of a God. That God is a Word made manifest. Perhaps this is the meaning of those words of the Christ that heaven and earth would pass away but that His "words" would never pass away. The heaven of our souls, and the earth of our bodies, continually change and pass. Says *The Voice of Silence*:

> Thy shadows [physical bodies] live and vanish; that which in thee shall live for ever, that which in thee knows (for it is knowledge) is not of fleeting life: it is the Man that was, that is, and will be, for whom the hour shall never strike.

It is a wonderful and striking thought that there is something unique, eternal, waiting to be said through every human soul. But it cannot be " said " until the soul and body are at-oned with the awakened Spirit. In *At the Feet of the Master*, it is put beautifully:

> He [the initiate] is as a pen in the hand of God, through which His thought may flow, and find for itself an expression down here, which without a pen it could not have.

The awakened Spirit in man, which becomes one with God or Life, becomes also the pure channel of that Life and Wisdom and Love.

Here we have the true meaning of the ancient doctrine of the Trinity. Here, again, if we look at ourselves, the microcosms, we shall understand the Macrocosm, God. On the side of matter as well as on the side of consciousness we are trinities. There is not a single form in this world that is not bounded by three dimensions, breadth, length and height. These three can be expressed mathematically as being at right angles to each other, as at the corner of a box, " in this Trinity none is afore, or after the other." The same is true of our powers of consciousness. We think, we feel, we act. We cannot help doing these three all the time, and who can tell where the one begins and the other ends. To what fulfilment, to what consummation, do they point? Thinking surely one day leads to Wisdom. All feelings can be placed on two sides: those which are derivatives of love, and those which spring from hate. All the love-emotions are creative, happiness-creating; those which spring from hate are mutually destructive. (This provides one of the finest arguments that Love lies at the root of the universe. Otherwise its " heavenly order " would have vanished long ago.) The only enduring feeling is Perfect Love.

Then again, our bodies, with their continual activity, the ever-recurring frustrations and inhibitions of physical matter, cause us continually to exert effort or strength. These lead to final mastery, to Adeptship, to limitless Power. Thus, behind the activities of mind and heart and body, we have an unfolding seed of perfect Wisdom, Love and Power—the Trinity which upholds the universe. *There* lie the immortal Wisdom, the unending Bliss, the Freedom of limitless Power—deep within ourselves, awaiting evocation and development. But that will only come when we have " lost " or destroyed our little, personal selves, for " the Spirit bloweth where it listeth ", and cannot be made the appanage of a tiny, personal self. Till that moment " only fragments of the great song " reach our ears, in our highest, purest, most self-forgetting moments, when, as unembodied joy, we stretch our soul's wings to fly.

Thus, life after life, the God in us atones for the " sins " of his personalities, looking forward to the time when the atonement will become the at-one-ment, and man becomes more than man.

The Spirit itself beareth witness with our spirit, that we are the children of God:

And if children, then heirs; heirs of God, and joint-heirs with Christ; if so be that we suffer with *him*, that we may be also glorified together.

For I reckon that the sufferings of this present time are not worthy to be compared with the glory which shall be revealed in us.

For the earnest expectation of the creature waiteth for the manifestation of the sons of God.

For the creature was made subject to vanity, not willingly, but by reason of him who hath subjected the same in hope,

Because the creature itself also shall be delivered from the bondage of corruption into the glorious liberty of the children of God.[1]

[1] *Romans*, 8.

CHAPTER V

GOD AND LIFE

WHAT is life? We spend it so recklessly and use it so ignorantly. All around us is life, instinct in every atom, in every breath, in all the vast universe. Everywhere it is the same Life—there is no other. And it clothes itself in innumerable forms—unending in their diversity and uniqueness. These two great principles of Life are immensely impressive, the unending unity of Life, and its extraordinary diversity of form, each form eternally unique, so that there are no two snowflakes exactly alike, nor two blades of grass.

If we look out on a starry night, at the unfathomable, unplumbable depths of space, the vast hosts of solar systems, star clusters and nebulae, the light of some only now reaching our eyes after centuries have passed, the mind reels at the thought of the unthinkable vastness of space! The greatest telescope can still only reveal to us the immensity of the universe, its unimaginable size. Even our little solar system, so small, so unimportant compared with many others, is placed alone in space, millions of miles from any other starry cluster. If the sun were reduced to a ball nine feet in diameter, the earth would be about the size of a pea, at which ratio the nearest star to our solar system would be 30,000 miles! What a lonely little system we are. No wonder the Blessed Damozel, leaning out from the gold bar of Heaven, saw the earth spin like a fretful midge. There are other systems, not too far away in this vast universe, which are enormously greater than ours, taking much vaster periods of time to revolve in their respective orbits. How vast! How vast is God! There is no end to His Immensity.

There is also no end to His Littleness. Never will a microscope be discovered which will bring us to the end of the hidden life of the universe.

> Whither shall I go from thy spirit, or whither shall I flee from thy presence? If I ascend up into heaven, thou art there; if I make my bed in hell, behold, thou art there. If I take the wings of the morning, and dwell in the uttermost parts of the sea; even there shall thy hand lead me, and thy right hand shall hold me. . . . The darkness and the light are both alike to thee. (*Psalm* 139)

Yet regard the order, the beauty, the harmony of it all. No system interferes with another system. No world, or system of worlds, but runs its appointed course. The heavenly order is indeed "a thing of beauty and a joy for ever". The great Architect of the Universe is so perfect an Artist that He fashions the most minute and unseen form as perfectly as any other.

Let us consider first the unity of the universe, that all-embracing, all-pervading Life and Consciousness. For all life is conscious. Consciousness is only another name for Life, though it may not be the *mental* consciousness which we associate with ourselves. That One Life, that One Consciousness—has it One Will, One Motive? Yes, one part of the Will of God is the direction in which the universe is travelling, and in the succession of events. I once read an article by a great scientist in America, and he said we could never realize the tremendous speed at which the universe was travelling all in one direction! To quote the well-known lines of Tennyson:

> One God, one law, one element,
> And one far-off divine event,
> To which the whole creation moves.

God is Love. Love is the only constructive, creative force in the universe. There is no other. Its temporary opposite, hate, is mutually destructive and death-dealing. The universe *must* be founded on Love, or it would not hold together for another minute. But what is Love? It is something far greater, nobler, wiser, than the petty self-satisfying emotion men signify by that name. One of the fundamental crimes of the universe is to take life, for we cannot give life or restore it, and so we become petty thieves of God.

Let us consider the wonder of its multiplicity and variety when clothed in form, and its inviolable uniqueness. Not for God is the regimentation beloved of man, but a scrupulous respect for the integrity and uniqueness of every form. Casting off one form, and entering into others that are new, the advancing stream of life ever retains its own indestructible uniqueness.

I have spoken of "God", but so often the word connotes so many cruel and ungodlike attributes. We may call Him by many names: the Heart of the Universe; the Eternal Beauty, for true Beauty, like true Love, is so much more than what passes under that name; the Undying Life; the Ageless Wisdom; the Underlying Arms of Love. Many, many are His Names. In our littleness we attribute to Him our own form and qualities, but our conception of Him grows with our growth. The great sceptic, Voltaire, once said:

> In the beginning God created man in His own image, and man has been returning Him that compliment ever since.

Only one thing is there to do, to try to gain the sense of the immensity and unity of Life, for that will save us from many sorrows. " God is Life," says Dr. S. Radhakrishnan, " recognition of this fact is spiritual consciousness." Science has re-discovered God. Scientists now say that there is evidence of a Master Mind behind the universe, and that as far as they can understand it, it appears to be a great mathematician.

Life never ceases to be, but it also never ceases to move, the Is and the Ever-Becoming. There is no such thing in reality as the Present. There is only the Future unceasingly becoming the Past. H. P. Blavatsky tells us that the sensation of the Present is produced by a blur on the consciousness similar to the blur produced on the retina of the eye by a lighted taper being swung in a circle, creating an illusory wheel of fire. The whole universe is in ceaseless, rhythmic movement, the " eternal motion " that is God in action. It clothes itself in a succession of events, all of them causally connected or related. This succession of events passes us for the most part unheeded and not understood. Yet what is it in reality? Has it any enduring message or significance? The East calls this unceasing chain of cause and effect, Karma. It is really the *Will of God in action*, and presages only, in the long run, final good.

Time, said Albert Einstein, is the fourth dimension to three-dimensional space. We can only picture what lies behind yesterday or what is ahead of tomorrow. But there is a condition of consciousness in which the illuminated seer, one with Life, lives in the Eternal Now, and for him time and space have vanished. " For a thousand years in thy sight are but as yesterday."

But time and space to us are very valid realities, and the majestic sequence of events unfolds under universal and stupendous Law. Every living thing, from the may-fly to a universe, has its life-cycle. In all Nature there is a never-ceasing rhythm. A voice speaking to our ears causes rhythmic undulations in the air. The eyes perceive a myriad rhythmic undulations in the ether.

The whole of evolution may be summed up in this way, the response from within, and the gradual organization of the organs of that response to the repeated impacts from without. Gradually, gradually, the hidden consciousness responds, unfolds, develops. It is the soul itself, said Cicero, which sees and hears, and not those parts which are, as it were, but windows to the soul.

Here we touch upon another wonderful principle of the universe, that every form of life begins in a tiny beginning, a cell, a seed, an atom. Yet within that tiny beginning is held all the promise and potency of what is afterwards revealed. Never can any form of life become other than what it fundamentally is. The Ever-Becoming is always what it Is. "To every seed his own body," said St. Paul. Just as an acorn holds within it the future giant of the forest, the germ-cell the future man, so each soul has its own peculiar destiny and path. "Become that which you are," said St. Ambrose to his people.

The growth of any life proceeds in cycles, not by a direct road, but by a concatenation of cycles, bearing the endless chain of cause and effect. Through cycles of day and night, birth and death, life proceeds to its "far-off divine event". As with may-flies and men, so is it with planets and solar systems, even a universe. *The Vishnu Purana* dramatically describes the coming on of the "night" of a planet which rivals in intensity Coleridge's "Last Man". But such immensities do not practically concern us.

> Who knows the secret? Who proclaimed it here?
> Whence, whence this manifold creation sprang?
> The most High Seer that is in highest heaven,
> He knows it—or perchance even he knows not.
>
> *Rig Veda*

> Ere the foundations of the earth were laid,
> Thou wert. And when the subterranean same
> Shall burst its prison and devour the flame,
> Thou shalt be still as thou wert there before
> And know no change when time shall be no more;
> O endless Thought, divine Eternity!
>
> *Gazing into Eternity*

CHAPTER VI

WHY ARE WE HERE?

THIS question has to a slight extent been already answered in the foregoing chapters. Sometimes towards the end of life people begin to wonder whether they have done all they meant to do in life. Before the world wars devastated the world, there used to be correspondence in the papers on the subject, "Is life worth living?" Looked at from a purely material standpoint, life with all its worries, disappointments and frustrations would hardly seem worth it, but from a spiritual view it is seen to have a glorious goal and purpose. To quote again St. Paul:

> For I reckon that the sufferings of this present time are not worthy to be compared with the glory which shall be revealed in us.

In fact, only the spiritual outlook can give us the romance and joy of living. It may be that some look back and remember the ideals and ambitions of youth, and realize how far short of them they fell. "Ah! but a man's reach should exceed his grasp," wrote Robert Browning, "or what's a heaven for?" But did we really come here to acquire a fortune, mount the social scale, or see our name going down to posterity? At the gateway of death all these must be surrendered. We cannot take them with us. Then, for what did we come? I suggest that we look in a new direction for the answer.

We came here and put on the working-clothes, the " school-uniform ", of the body, in order to come into touch with the order of experience to be gained here, and which is veritably the food for our soul's growth. It is the soul that matters most, not the body, and its growth shows as increasing, inherent character and capacity. Does life teach us nothing? Surely, we would grow a great deal more swiftly, if we could only understand life. If, towards its close, we could look back and see that we have grown in understanding, patience, sympathy, tolerance, then surely we have not lived in vain; for these are " treasures in heaven " which we *can* take away with us through the gateway of death, and bring back again with us through the gateway of the next birth.

This leads me to the method by which our souls steadily grow. This life is not the only one we live in the great School of Life. It is a Day in our soul's long journey; we have lived through many such days or lives before, and shall live through many yet.

Now, there are two things of " intuition " to be noted here. One is man's ineradicable belief in his own immortality. Even savages have that belief. Such a widespread belief must have some foundation in fact. Man has this faith or belief. But what is " faith "?

It is not a mere ability to " believe " something contrary to reason. There is no " gift of faith ". A Master of the Wisdom has defined it as " the soul's unlearned knowledge ", a deep intuition beyond reason and experience. Here man is clearly right.

The other intuition to be noted is man's inherent belief in progress. Very few of us honestly believe that things will not one day get better. Some persons unthinkingly picture progress as a straight road up which all humanity has to do is to walk. Now I believe that there is no such thing as a really straight line anywhere in the universe. Everything moves in cycles, both in time and space. The oldest universal symbol is the circle, and the ancient Greeks said that progress proceeded in a spiral, history continually repeating itself upon a higher level.

This is equally true of both space and time. Wherever we move in this world we are always at the centre of a perfect circle, clearly to be seen during a sea voyage. But mentally we are also the centre of a circle centripetal and centrifugal, receiving a variety of impressions and sending a variety out into infinity. Then, did we ever know an evening that did not turn again to another morning, or a winter that never turned to another spring? Why should we stop there? What about the cycle of a man's life? It follows the same immutable law as the cycle of a day. His youth is the early morning, positive and vigorous, growing steadily towards maturity or midday. There will come a time when invisibly, imperceptibly, the tide of life will turn and begin to flow towards the evening of life. This becomes increasingly more negative, satiated, saturated with experience, and towards its close a very beautiful and wonderful thing takes place. The spiritual Self, approaching the evening of life, begins a synthetic process, a summing up of his life's experiences. For this, his soul and body should have peace. There are two things often to be seen in our topsy-turvy civilization today, youth without hope—whilst youth needs ambition, hope, adventure—and old age without peace.

Have we noticed the lovely peace that falls over the earth like a blessing as the sun goes down? In the East, where they have a story for everything, they say that at that moment the four Devarājas or Regents meet, and bless the earth. There is also a force radiating from the centre of the earth which up to midday is positive, looking to inner vision as a rosy light. After midday this radiation slowly turns blue, like a piece of litmus paper, and negative. Therefore the morning hours are best for all positive, creative work, also for the writing of important letters; after midday the judgment of most of us is not quite so clear, and we can be more sentimental then.

Are we afraid to fall asleep when night comes? No, because we know that we shall come back in the morning and pick up the threads of life again just where we laid them down the night before. The same principle rules our lives. When we "die" we pass g rest-time of the Spirit, during which we ate all the experiences of life. When that process is completed, it is time for *tanha*, the "thirst for sentient existence", to arise in the soul, and this will inevitably lead him back to another life. It was stated that life's experiences are the food for our soul's growth. To keep that rough simile for a moment, compare it with what happens to our physical bodies. The food we eat becomes the physical "us". We may be half-an-hour taking a square meal, but we shall be many hours digesting or assimilating it, and then it will have become part of our bodies, and we shall become hungry for more. In a similar but more spiritual sense, life's experiences are the food for our soul's growth. We may be three-score years and ten taking it, but we shall be hundreds of years, as we count time here, assimilating it, and then it will have become the psychological "us", showing here as character and aptitudes, and we shall be "hungry" to return to another life.

Thus do we grow life after life in the great School of Life. We speak of clever and cultured people having "more in them"; what we really mean is that more power and capacity has been unfolded and evinced in such people, for every one has *everything* in potentiality deep within him. Life is truly an *education*, which word does not mean putting or cramming something into a child's head which was not there before, but gently and patiently "leading out" into expression latent and undeveloped power.

This will be clearly seen if we study contrasting types of men. What does life mean to the undeveloped peasant and to the poet or philosopher? What does a glorious sunset mean to a simple peasant? That it will be fine for the crops in the morning. What does it mean to the soul of a poet? "Thoughts that do often lie too deep for tears."

A happy savage takes so little and such elementary experience from life that he may come back in fifty or a hundred years; the simple peasant in three hundred years. The ordinary civilized person needs anything from five hundred to eight hundred years; whilst the soul of a Plato, an Albert Einstein, a Shakespeare may well need two thousand years to assimilate all they have achieved on earth. H. P. Blavatsky has stated that Plato has not yet come back.

This, again, leads us to another truth. It has been stated that all men are fundamentally "Sons of the Most High". On this tremendous truth rests its necessary corollary, the Brotherhood of Man. Here again, let us observe that Nature's rules are few, continually repeated on greater or lesser levels. Was there ever a family where every one was the same age? What a dull world it would be if they were! Just the same truth is to be seen in the great family of humanity. No one here is the same soul-age. Some have lived so much longer in the School of Life than others, and therefore are wiser, cleverer, more spiritual, they have "more in them", which means, as has been stated, more unfolded from within, more expressed.

Roughly speaking, we may classify humanity like the classes in a school. First, there is the "kindergarten", in which we can place the simple savage peoples. Like children they have little power of concentration, are not fond of long hours of labour, like to sing and dance and play, are devoted to "fairy stories". Life would be easier for all if their conquerors realized this and gave them more kindness and patience. For the extinction of primitive races means that it will result in their taking birth in the lower ranks of their conquerors, creating dire social problems.

Rising in the scale we come to the simple peasantry of civilized countries. These for the most part constitute the "lower classes" in the School of Life.

Next come what we call civilized ranks, if there is such a thing yet as true civilization. (True civilization is not a question of more motor cars, better plumbing, etc. It is a question of innate culture, of a background of soul-growth.)

I think we may divide the vast mass of civilized people, the "higher classes" of the School of Life, into two main divisions, a distinction clearly to be seen in the "classless" population of the United States. There is the majority stratum, composed of good, honest, kind people, but souls of limited views and small outlook. They can understand vividly the question of "what happens to me, my family, my friends, my home town," etc. What happens to the nation is a thought that occurs but seldom, and what happens to humanity, hardly at all. On the other hand a minority stratum *does* care, can envisage the outlook of the nation and humanity at large. We may call them the "idealists" who are the salt of the earth. They are capable of self-abnegation and self-sacrifice for a larger ideal than their own immediate surroundings.

From their ranks come the great, outstanding figures of every nation: great saints, statesmen, leaders, artists, scientists, philosophers. These already transcend the boundaries of the nation which gave them birth, and belong to the world, for Shakespeare, Michael Angelo, Plato, Abraham Lincoln, St. Francis, Beethoven, etc. are now the precious heritage of all nations equally. Passing out of the School of Life, they form special classes of Adepts, to be described in a later chapter.

This is the great truth of Reincarnation, which is fast coming back to the western world. It must not be confused with the idea of transmigration according to which the soul of a man may inhabit an animal body. The soul of a man cannot do that. It has passed a barrier which cannot be gone back upon, as a child cannot re-enter his mother's womb and be born again.

This provokes the question, have animals souls and do they live after death? The difference between an animal and man is that an animal is a duality, it has a "soul" or psychic counterpart which lives for some time after death, and is then absorbed into the "Group-Soul" of its species; whilst man is a trinity of body, soul, and immortal, undying Spirit, who can never return to a lower stage of evolution. This will be more fully described in another chapter.

The truth of Reincarnation at once throws light upon the complex problems of human life. Without it, as ancient Hierocles said, it is impossible to justify the ways of God to man. For centuries the Christian world lost this saving truth, and so was forced to the illogical position of placing unending results upon fleeting and finite causes. We are taught that when a baby is born a quite new soul is created to live in that body, that upon this short and fleeting life rests a whole eternity of bliss or woe for ever and ever and ever. Now we cannot have eternity at one end of the stick only. If we are now going to live for ever we have already lived for ever and ever. And, if that unbelievable hypothesis could possibly be true, who will explain to us how a Creator who is Love, gave to one man so much in the way of heredity, parentage and surroundings, and to another man so little that we sometimes say of him: "Poor fellow, he never had a chance from the very beginning."

The differences between men are far wider than they are in any other kingdom of Nature. Observe the wide difference in mental development between a simple savage, a moronic child, and the brain of a Plato, an Albert Einstein. All the training in the world will not make the one the equal of the other. The same difference shows in the world of the emotions. What worlds apart are the cruel, predatory instincts, the utter absence of compassion and good-will in a Bill Sykes, and the selfless, world-embracing tenderness and compassion of a Saint Francis. Even in the sphere of action the same thing is to be seen. There are some people who never can do things right; if asked to lay a table they will put the knives and forks crookedly upon it. Compare these with great men of action and powers of organization, great statesmen, leaders, business heads.

In old days we were told not to inquire, we were not " meant to know ". But if we *can* know, we are surely meant to know. Why otherwise did the Christ tell men to seek and they would find? For what other purpose do we possess an intelligence and the spirit of inquiry? Yes, we were told, God's ways are past finding out. It is impious to inquire.

But the answer is clear. Powers of mind and heart, and even environment, are not the arbitrary gifts of an almighty God. They represent a long past of gradual development. The savage and cruel man will one day in the far future become the Saint; the ineffective person, the great man of affairs; the dullard the man of mind. We shall describe the laws under which this is achieved in the next chapter. Meanwhile it can be seen that Reincarnation is a doctrine of Hope. There is no ideal that lights the human heart that cannot be achieved *in time*. " All I could never be, all men ignored in me, this, was I worth to God, whose wheel the pitcher shaped." (R. Browning.) It means too that injuries done to others, mistakes made by ourselves, will all be rectified in time and *by ourselves*, not even by the vicarious power of a great and holy saviour. Is this not a truth of illimitable hope and a doctrine for true men?

It is entirely in line with the apparent principles of Nature that life continually repeats itself upon a higher level. Through this cyclic return to earth, the soul grows gradually towards its sublime destiny. Why should we suppose that our souls do not evolve, as our bodies do? William James once put it like this:

> Mind and matter have evolved together and are therefore somewhat of a mutual fit.

Not only does an individual soul reincarnate, but also the corporate soul of a nation. Where are the souls who once inhabited Greek, Roman, Chaldean and Egyptian bodies with their civilizations? They are here today, and similar traits can be observed in their modern representatives. The modern Briton is largely, though never entirely, a reincarnation of the ancient Roman. He has the same sense of law and order, the same liberal colonizing instinct over subject-peoples. The *pax Romana* has become the *pax Britannica*. The French are largely reincarnated Greeks. They have the sense of perfection, the quarrelling sense of individuality which the ancient Greeks possessed. And the Germans come largely from ancient Phoenicia, with its talent for industry and far-flung commercial undertakings. A certain proportion of them, particularly the ardent Nazis, are reincarnated Carthaginians, inheriting the same insensitive cruelty and hatred of their Roman conquerors. One day in the future there will be no British, German and French races, etc. left. They will belong to the myths of history. New races will have arisen, and are even now, in all the " new " countries, showing dawning characteristics.

Even a planet reincarnates, also a solar system, unthinkable as may be the periods of time involved. The ancient books of the East say that the whole universe does so too. They speak in dramatic terms of the " Days and Nights of Brahma ". It is a universal Law, the flow and ebb of Life, the ceaseless Motion which manifests itself in rhythmic cycles. From one standpoint everything can be reduced to different " wave-lengths ". I once saw a chart drawn up by a Parisian technical college. It enumerated the different " vibrations " known to science, all physical of course. It commenced with the lowest and slowest sound-waves travelling through the air. The higher notes of a piano, for instance, are incredibly quicker than the lower ones. Sound passes into inaudibility, not because it is no longer there, but because our ears are no longer able to register it. People are different here. I have heard that the squeak of a bat is so near the limit that some people cannot hear it. On the other hand, I once knew a musician whose hearing was so sensitive that when he pulled a string of his violincello he not only heard the note but its " over-tones " as well, what is called the harmonic chord of Nature.

After sound-waves come light-waves, enormously faster and finer and travelling not through the air but through the ether. These are caught by our eyes, and we call it "seeing". Here again we are very different. Some people, as some hill tribes in India, can see a difference between two shades of colour that are non-existent to others. The higher ranges of vibrations ended in the list in X-Rays and Gamma Rays, both of which are invisible to normal vision, but can be caught by a sensitive photographic plate. I noticed in that list several big vacua. Yet it is not to be supposed that there was really nothing there. There is a saying: "Nature abhors a vacuum." I do not believe that there is ever a real vacuum. In the words of an ancient Gnostic scripture:

> Nowhere is there an emptiness, but everywhere a conditioned fullness.

The most seemingly valid objection to the idea of reincarnation is that we do not seem to "remember". What do we mean by memory? Most people mean by it the ability to recall certain pictures or facts in the mind. This seems to depend upon the condition of the brain. When we get old or worn out we cannot remember so well. But if that is all that memory really consists of we have already "forgotten" the greater part of this life, nay, even the greater part of one day. If we were to sit down at night and try to recall every thought that had passed through our minds that day, every emotional reaction we had, every word and happening around us, how much would we "remember"? Yet psychology will tell us that no single tiny thought and event occurred but it made an indelible impression on the consciousness, even those events and happenings which seemed to be unobserved by the waking consciousness.

Our brain is a kind of clearing-house. Every impression passes through it to be registered by the inner psychic self, the soul. There it is never forgotten. From it come back fragmentary, seemingly forgotten episodes during unconsciousness under an anaesthetic or at the moment of death. But for practical purposes it comes back to us in daily life in a synthetic form. For instance, a musician does not "remember" all the thousands of times he practised. Yet Nature does, and gives it back to him as a capacity, a power.

Why should we suppose that this ceases with death? It comes back again with the soul to the next incarnation, showing as latent and inherent capacity. If all we try to learn and do in this life resulted only in an unending life where it was no earthly or heavenly use to us, what waste of time that would be! The growing synthesis is carried on from life to life.

Another aspect of it shows as "character", which means the result of brave or cowardly facing of life's problems, habitual thought-grooves having become established traits of character.

Yet another aspect consists of instinctive likes and dislikes. What makes us instinctively draw to some people and not to others? What causes the well-known phenomenon of falling in love at first sight? These come from the past, are the voices of our past speaking. With every succeeding life of friendship or relationship, the bond is strengthened. A wonderful example of this is the story of David and Jonathan. As soon as the prince saw the shepherd boy, despite the difference in social status of the two, the soul of Jonathan was knit to the soul of David and he loved him as his own soul. Why did he, when he knew nothing of him? Because it was the instant recognition of old friends from the past. Marriages that are " made in heaven " are another example. Such happily wedded couples have known and loved each other well before.

It must not be concluded that we always return in the same relationships or even the same sex. What is a relationship but an angle of loving? Have we not often seen a motherly attitude in a wife, or a fatherly one in a husband? Surely we shall love best those who mean most to us by learning to love them in all the ways of love and not only in one way. I remember a little boy of twelve who faithfully came to every one of a long series of lectures by myself in the town of Bradford. At the last he brought his pretty young mother.

" Jacky is so taken up with what you talk about," she told me, " and he says that next life he will be my father, so that he can look after me!" Perhaps he *had* been his mother's father already.

The idea of a change of sex is very strange to many people, generally, I am bound to confess, to the male side of life. But whilst we are in the body of a woman, we get an entirely different set of experiences, and quite different qualities are evolved in us, different yet complementary, to the other side of life. But do not the best examples on both sides show forth the finer characteristics of the other? Has not the finest man something of a woman's intuition and sympathy; the finest woman something of the resolution and strength of a man? Where did they develop them except by experience on both sides of life?

The general rule seems to be to enter upon a series of incarnations on one side of life and then to change over to a series on the other side. Does this explain something often to be noticed—a little girl who is a tom-boy, and a little boy who furtively wants to play with dolls? Perhaps they have just come over from a long series upon the other side of life. The Spirit in man is sexless, as the Christ told us when stating that in Heaven there is neither marriage nor giving in marriage. Perhaps it would be better to say that it contains the high essence of both.

Wrote Edgar Wallace in one of his novels:

> I thought the first time I saw Bones that he was a fool. I was wrong. Then I thought he was effeminate. I was wrong again, for he played the man whenever he was called upon to do so. He is one of

those rare creatures, a man with all the moral equipment of a good woman. " I think you have defined the perfect man," she said.

One more objection to reincarnation must be noted, and this is generally voiced by mothers. " What! " they will say, " do you mean to tell me that in the future, *my* child will be somebody else's child? " Now, a child does not *belong* to any of us personally. He belongs to himself and to Life. But he could not have come to us if love-links from the past had not drawn him to us.

Sometimes, though this may not be stressed as its cause may occur in this life, an incurable phobia comes from another life. Death under torture, or in circumstances of great fear, can create a " memory " which persists into another life.

Yet, too, vivid picture-memories of the past *do* come back. Rudyard Kipling describes a hypothetical case of this in his famous story of the banker's clerk who remembered having been a galley-slave in Rome. The writer has heard many such tales, but then she has been in a favourable position to hear them. Long years ago, when temporarily acting as Librarian at the Theosophical Headquarters in London, a wild young Irishman burst in and told her how he remembered a life as a gladiator in Rome. That man is now a famous writer and occultist.

Vivid pictures of the past seem to come back in two ways; either in the form of a continually recurring dream, or as a vision in the waking mind. A good example of the dream form was recounted to the writer after a lecture on Reincarnation in Bristol, England. A young tram-car conductor in his uniform came up to her and said: "You have explained a dream I have had all my life. In this dream I am in a house with white pillars with several other men, all of us in white togas with red borders. I suppose I am remembering a life in ancient Greece?" "No," I replied, remembering enough history to place it, "I think it was in ancient Rome, for only the patrician order which composed the Roman senate had the right to wear the red-bordered toga."

Here before me was the reincarnation of a Roman noble and I have often been asked whether he had "come down" in evolution in this life? Now I do not think evolution regards our social distinctions in the same way as we do, but I imagine something like this. Nowhere in all the world was it possible to have the proverbial "good time" as it was in ancient Rome. Perhaps this nobleman did not take the duties of his caste seriously, but wasted his substance in riotous living. Therefore in this life he is born where he must work hard. Will that do him any harm?

But the most wonderful waking vision of a past life was told me in London, again after a lecture on Reincarnation. An elderly lady stepped up to me, "My dear," she said, "I have never heard anyone speak on Reincarnation before, but I believe you. Let me tell you why. Many years ago when I was passing through a sad and troubled time in life, I was just about to get into bed one night when suddenly a queer light filled my room, my bedroom in London disappeared and I found myself in a Roman house, and clothed in the robes of a Roman lady. Holding my hand was a little girl of twelve, whom I recognized as again my daughter in this present life. All round me were grouped the slaves of the household, but we were all in a state of terrible fear. The air was dark and full of dust and falling ashes."

From something she observed she found out afterwards that this was taking place during the destruction of ancient Herculaneum, not Pompeii. It will be remembered that fewer escaped from Herculaneum than Pompeii when Vesuvius suddenly erupted, because it was much nearer the mountain. "We could not escape, we were waiting for death," she went on. "Suddenly there came into the room a man friend bringing with him two little vials of a powerful poison, that my child and I might die a more merciful death." And those who have seen the plaster casts of victims overtaken by the boiling lava tide can picture what kind of death they thus sought to avoid. "I gave my child one draught and she died in my arms. Then I prepared to take the second one myself, when one of the slave-girls in an agony of terror appealed to me to let her have it. So I gave it to the girl, and I suppose I died in the ordinary manner but by then I was coming back to my room in London and the other scene was disappearing."

I remember a little Irishwoman waiting in the rain to catch me after a lecture in Dublin. "Oh! Miss," she said, "you have explained what they used to beat me for saying, when I was little, that I remembered the house I had lived in before. But I did, Miss, I did! I remember that it had no glass in the windows (a mediaeval house would have no glass!) And, oh! Miss, I want to thank you because you have taken away the fear of death from me."

Sometimes children remember, and the memory fades out as they grow up. The most striking case of this came to me whilst lecturing in the Channel Islands. In the audience was a South African lady who was now living in Jersey. She asked me to come home with her and spend the night. Then I heard what she wished to tell me. She had a little boy, born in Jersey, who, when alone playing with his Teddy-bear, talked quite intelligible Zulu to it. "Now," she said, "I know Zulu because I was born and brought up in S. Africa, but how does he know it?"

Then I told her of a beautiful truth, how quite often a child who dies before it is seven years old, about which age the immortal Ego takes complete control of the body, returns almost at once to earth, and quite often to the same father and mother as a younger child. "Did you ever," I asked her, "have another child before him?" "Yes," she replied, "when I was first married in S. Africa, but he died." "Do you not see," I said, "that he has come back to you, and has even brought back some memory of the language he talked with the Zulu servants?"

I have told this true story to learned professors. Some of them have discoursed to me about " ancestral memory ". But to me the answer is clear and only reincarnation can give it.

This truth is natural to unperverted man. Has not a child often asked his mother: " Mummy, where was I before I came here? " Because it is natural and known deep within us, it comes intuitively to many a philosopher, such as the German writers, Schopenhauer, Lessing and Fichte, and the Scotch philosopher, McTaggart, and to the poets most of all, perhaps because the intuition of the poet soars into the empyrean and pierces into Plato's world of the Divine Ideation. The great poet of Reincarnation is Robert Browning. Every one will recall his poem, *Evelyn Hope*, and that in which he writes that he cannot carve statues or paint pictures: " This of verse alone one life allows me. Other heights in other lives, God willing." Dante Gabriel Rossetti has a famous little poem beginning " I have been here before." I even found a reference to reincarnation in the puritanical Milton in his sonnet, *On the death of a fair infant.* " Wert thou that just maid," he writes, " who once before, forsook the hated earth . . . and camest again to visit me once more? " But then it must be remembered that Milton was a student of the old Jewish esoteric scripture, the Zohar.

It may be objected: Does Christianity teach it? Is it mentioned in the Bible? There is no other explanation for the statement of the Christ to His disciples that

John the Baptist *was* " Elias, which was for to come." If He did not explain this specific doctrine to the populace it was because they already saw life from that point of view (*vide* the disciples' question about the man being born blind), as Josephus, the Jewish historian, tell us. References may even be found in the Old Testament. In the Apocrypha there is a reference to a good soul which was therefore given a good body; and there is the famous saying of the Prophet Jeremiah that even before he was born, whilst yet his members, were not formed, God knew him and ordained him to be a prophet unto the nations.

The early Christian Church had that teaching. It was well known among the esoteric sects of the Gnostics or Knowers. But when the uneducated mass of the people submerged the Church the teaching was lost. At a Church Council in Constantinople, in the sixth century under the Emperor Justinian, a resolution was passed that those who held the heretical doctrine of the soul's pre-existence and the consequent wonderful opinion of its return were *anathema*. Thus passed this saving truth for man for many centuries from the Christian Faith; but not entirely, for esoteric and heretical sects have held and taught it through the centuries, amongst them the ancient Rosicrucians and the Cambridge Platonists who included amongst their numbers the saintly Sir Thomas More.

Among other great men in the past who knew the truth of the cyclic return of the soul to earth was Benjamin Franklin, who came into touch early in life with the occult side of life. He gaily wrote an *Epitaph for himself*:

The Body of
Benjamin Franklin, printer,
(Like the cover of an old book,
Its contents worn out,
And stript of its lettering, and gilding)
Lies here, food for worms!
Yet the work itself shall not be lost,
For it will, as he believed, appear once more
In a new
And more beautiful edition,
Corrected and amended
By its Author!

CHAPTER VII

HOW WE CREATE OUR DESTINIES

WHAT governs our destinies? Most people seem to attribute what they call fate to inscrutable heavenly powers, the prevailing social system, or their own personal heredity and upbringing. None of these are casual or happen by chance. In reality there is simply no such thing as chance or luck anywhere in the universe. All is the result of seen or unseen, known or not understood, *Law*. In religious parlance we talk about the Will of God and the Commandments of God, but what are they in reality?

I think we may define the Will of God as the "increasing purpose" of the universe. On a certain very high and subtle plane it can even be "seen"; and there it is a mighty, shining tide, resistless in its onward march. Astronomers have told us how the universe is moving with tremendous speed in one main direction. Emerson, a student of the ancient Upanishads of India, has described it as moving towards the final beatitude and fulfilment of every living thing. The foundation Law of the universe is Love, and it is slowly but surely moving towards bliss and power.

And what are the "Commandments" of God? We surely no longer think they are ten in number written upon tablets of stone and given to Moses on the top of a mountain. The Commandments of God are the great and unalienable Laws of Nature. H. P. Blavatsky has described them as " the impress of the Divine Mind upon matter ". They express the Mind of God, and in the poetic words of scripture, " with whom is no variableness, neither shadow of turning "; He is " the same yesterday, and today, and for ever ". This beautifully describes the workings of all the Laws of Nature. Given the same conditions they eternally re-act in the same way. They did it millions of years ago, they will millions of years hence. Hence we may say without irreverence that God, the Creative Life, does not change His Mind.

These things are better depicted by the poetry of religious writings than by the matter-of-fact phraseology of science. Yet science and religion are not opposed. They mutually complement each other, like the right and left hands of a man. Science approaches truth from below, by patient investigation and deduction; religion is the artistic approach, using the flight of the intuition and its consequent poetic symbolism and hyperbole. Yet, as George Sand said: "The mind seeks, but it is the heart which finds."

Every Law of Nature, every event, is the Voice of God speaking to us. If we obey that Voice the result is happiness and expansion. To disobey, however ignorantly, means limitation, sorrow, death. This is a new way of understanding the old words: " The soul that sinneth, it shall die." Quite useless is it to say that if a man is ignorant of a law, it is unfair that he should suffer. Nature acts according to its inherent being, quite regardless of any personal factor; and the sufferer will learn by the result. In fact the laws of Life were never yet broken. No one can break them. Those who run against them can only temporarily break themselves.

How important, then, that we should know, understand and obey them! Are we not in the School of Life just for that very purpose? We are slowly becoming law-conscious. The popularization of science has helped us here. We no longer regard the phenomena of Nature as the personal utterances of some God. Something of this superstitious attitude still lingers in country places. When I was a child, we lived next door to a farm, and the farmer was a man who habitually used very lurid language. One day a bull got him in the corner of a yard and badly gored him. I heard my nurse talking it over with our young cook. "Yes," she said, "when the bull got him he was swearing something dreadful. It's a judgment on him. He has been struck down." As if God were a kind of superior policeman, waiting to strike down those who swore!

But that frame of mind is disappearing. One aspect of Law which is becoming familiar to us is the growing knowledge of the "laws of health". What happens when we obey them? We reap physical vigour, relief and joy. What when we disobey them? Misery, disease and death. Sometimes it takes years before the final results appear, but it is looming nearer all the time. Be sure, your sin will find you out.

Now is it reasonable to think that whilst there are evident physical laws, there are not psychological and spiritual ones also? These are subtle, more far-reaching than their physical counterparts, and even affect to some extent the physical body and its environment too.

Let us study their effects on the inner and outer reaches of ourselves, and then we shall discover why we are as we are and why too we have a particular environment.

First of all I wish to say that we usually approach this question of ourselves and our destinies from too short and too superficial a standpoint. What do I mean by "from too short a standpoint"? Let us put it in another way. Imagine that we thought we only had this twenty-four hours to live, because we had forgotten that we had any yesterdays, and so, of course, we would not think that we were going to have any tomorrows. How still more incomprehensible life would then look! No one would set out upon any great undertaking, for what can be done in twenty-four hours? We would see children and old people and would not realize that one day the children would become the old people. We would probably think that they belonged to another order of creation.

What lends dignity, purpose, meaning to today? Its connection with other days which have preceded it and which will follow it. The greater a man's purpose the more days it takes to achieve it. The same principle is true of the " days " of our great soul-journey we call " life ". It acquires meaning, dignity and purpose in relation to other lives preceding and following it. The " romance " of life resides in its immortal spiritual meaning as Count Hermann Keyserling once observed.

Then, again, we look at things from too superficial a point of view when we regard mainly this body and its happenings and surroundings. But man is far more than that, far deeper than that. Are not his thoughts, his emotions, his spiritual aspirations even greater and more formative powers than those of his actions? In fact, man is a dynamo of tremendous power, though for the most part he does not realize it, radiating creative energy on three planes of matter simultaneously, by his thoughts, his desires and his actions.

If we were told that our actions did not matter for they would produce no particular result, we would not believe it, because we can *see* they do, even though we may not always be sure what kind of result they will produce. Is it not only reasonable to suppose that our thoughts and desires are producing equally, if not more, potent results? We cannot stop that continual action on our part, and the corresponding reaction of Nature, from going on unceasingly, because we can never stop thinking and feeling and acting. The thread of man's life is like that of three-ply wool. It has these three strands inextricably mingled, weaving the pattern of his future and his fate.

For the purpose of clarity in understanding we will mentally separate the three strands for a moment and study the specific action of each. But before commencing that let us observe another fact in Nature. We are so accustomed to think of our individual fate alone, as if it had nothing to do with anyone else. But what a man thinks and does and what happens to him is affecting many other people at the same time. " For none of us liveth to himself, and no man dieth to himself "—or even thinketh or feeleth to himself alone. We may regard corporate human destiny as a great carpet being woven into a beautiful design. We cannot well see what that design is yet, because we *are* the threads and are down in the thick of it. Perhaps if we were in the position of the " Gods ", right up above it, we would see what pattern was working out, as a man sees the relationships the streets of a town bear to each other when ascending a hill near by. Says a commentary on *Light on the Path*:

> The initiate has a right to demand the secrets of Nature and to know the rules which govern human life. He obtains this right by having escaped from the limits of Nature and by having freed himself from the rules which govern human life. He has become a recognized portion of the divine element, and is no longer affected by that which is temporary. He then obtains the knowledge of the laws which govern temporary conditions.

There are two other questions to be answered before we attempt to unravel the threefold cord of fate which guides and makes up our being. First, when we come back to earth we find ourselves born into a certain nation. Why? A nation is a "class" in the School of Life. Whilst we are in that class a certain side of us is being pre-eminently developed. For instance, if we are born amongst the more northern races of Europe our mental nature is receiving a slightly greater stimulus than if we had been born in the south where the emotional nature is more to the fore. In the long journey of the soul we pass through many nations and so an all-round development is assured. This is the answer to the prevalent over-emphasis of national consciousness in the world today. To destroy or stamp out a national culture, to impose an alien culture upon a subject-people, is to render the world poorer. There is a right and a wrong patriotism. The wrong form is the spirit of "my nation, right or wrong", my nation above all others. This can easily be seen to be absurd when we remember how many different national cultures we have already lived through. The right patriotism is to inquire, what is the peculiar genius of a nation which can be placed at the service of all the others?

Then, again, we find ourselves born into a certain family; why? There is an old saying that "we choose our friends, but God gives us our relations". Perhaps quite a number of people are in the position of a little boy who, one day, when he was very annoyed with his people, said: "I wish I had known what a horrible family I was coming to and then I never would have come!" We come because strong links from the past are drawing us once again into relationship. When a child is born we greet the "little stranger". But it never is a little stranger! A soul could not have come to our care unless love-links—and sometimes hate-links—for love and hate are both attractive forces—were not drawing him from the past. As stated before, this truth is again the answer to the prevalent problem of possessive motherhood. A child does not belong to us. We do not possess him. We do not even "form his character", for that was in process of forming long ago. The much more lovely way to look at it is this: he comes to us because we knew and loved him in the past, and so comes to our care whilst his body is still young and weak. Let us not try to impose our own ideas and will upon a growing child, but try intuitively to discern that which his own divine Ego wishes and intends.

Let us now unravel the threefold cord of fate that we may distinguish how each strand acts, and we will begin with the deepest, most far-reaching one of the three, that of thought.

Man is created by thought, made and conditioned by it. The very word "man" comes from a Sanskrit word which means "the thinker". Said the Lord Buddha: "Creatures from mind their character derive; mind-marshalled are they, mind-made. Mind is the source of either bliss or corruption." This same idea is voiced by both Epictetus and Shakespeare. Epictetus said that it was not so much the events of life that mattered, but what we *thought* about those events.

And the poet Shakespeare writes: "There is nothing either good or bad, but thinking makes it so." Thought is a vibration or wave-length in the mental strata of our souls and its surrounding atmosphere. A wave-length in our mental selves is at once communicated to the surrounding mental atmosphere. Who can tell how far the influence of a thought may reach?

"Beautiful it is to understand and know," wrote Carlyle, "that a thought did never yet die; that as man, the originator thereof, has gathered it and created it from the whole Past, so thou wilt transmit it to the whole Future."

And Francis Thompson wrote, with poetic licence:

All things by immortal power,
Near or far,
Hiddenly
To each other linked are,
That thou canst not stir a flower
Without troubling of a star.

This is such an important subject that we will devote the next chapter to it. Meanwhile we may express the power of our thinking in a kind of aphorism: *Thought creates character and capacities.*

It is quite easy to see how thinking forms our capacities, for if we never thought about what we were trying to do our power would not grow much. What is the result of a musician practising day after day, a business man spending years learning the elements of his calling, a judge or doctor or writer dealing year after year with human nature and its problems? A power grows, an experience grows, an understanding grows. When a man dies, what happens to that capacity? Does he now live in a world where it will be of no use? No, he takes that developed capacity with him and brings it back with him through the gateway of the next birth. There it may begin to show early in life, and people will say: "What a clever child; he should be taught so-and-so." If this process extends through many lives, that soul may one day be born as a genius, doing by the light of nature what other men strive after with slow pains. A genius is sometimes lop-sided in development, wonderful along one line and primitive along another. Perhaps most men develop in a more all-round fashion.

Great saints are spiritual geniuses, as was shown early in the lives, for example, of St. Teresa of Avila, and St. Thérèse of Lisieux. The genius of Mozart showed amazingly early in life, composing sonatas and symphonies at an age when most children are in the nursery.

If it be objected that the Law of Heredity explains all this, we will reply that heredity leaves as much unexplained as seemingly explained. It does not explain how genius rarely hands on its supreme power to its progeny. The sons of great men are proverbially less in stature than their fathers. Nor does it explain how a genius is found in the most unpropitious surroundings, and a "black-sheep" suddenly appears in a very reputable family.

The Law of Reincarnation does not negate the Law of Heredity, but covers and includes it as the greater includes the less. All that we inherit from our fathers and mothers is the type of instrument, i.e. brains and nervous system, upon which we, the consciousness, play; but the power to play on it is where we are our own ancestors. A man may be a very fine musician, but if he must perform upon an inferior piano, perhaps broken and with several notes that will not sound, he cannot evince much of his skill. The inferior instrument may be the result of heredity or accident. The limitation is the same, and is the result of past actions.

We may read the ancient Jewish Commandment in that light, that the " sins " of our past bear fruit until the succeeding third or fourth incarnation.

The limitation of the instrument is often felt, when people are aware of a difficulty in expressing their thoughts and interior intimations. It may be they neglected such opportunities in the past, and must strive harder now. Or it may be that circumstances are so placed that a desired development cannot be followed, and a less congenial one is forced upon one. That may mean that another side, a balancing feature, needs development. It is always wisest to make the best of every situation and circumstance since that attitude improves matters in the future. To make the worst of it is to add mounting and increasing difficulties. An Adept once wrote: " We try to make the best of the worst."

What is perhaps not so easy to see is that thought also creates character. Character is even more important than capacity, for do we not often see how men of great gifts waste them and their opportunities through sheer lack of character; and, again, how a man of mediocre attainments and opportunity will rise triumphant through strong and great character? Indeed we might borrow the old story of the good fairies who came to the birthday of the princess, each to give her a gift, and then an evil fairy who threw a spanner into the works too. What would we ask of Life—many mental gifts, wealth and secure surroundings? Let us ask the greatest gift of all, a strong and noble character, and that is in our own hands to make now and for the future. For the traits of character are only strongly established grooves of thought; an old saying puts it thus:

> Sow a thought, and you reap a tendency;
> Sow a tendency, and you reap a character;
> Sow a character, and you reap a destiny.

Character can be altered and transformed. We do not inherit our characters from our parents. They provide us with a certain facility to express characteristics similar to their own; for instance, a musical child may be born into a musician's family as thus he will be provided with the necessary sensitive nervous organization. Then there is the tremendous influence of mental and physical surroundings in childhood also to be considered. But how mind-power can be developed, how character may be transformed, will be described in the succeeding chapter.

Then there is the strand of feeling, emotion, desire. What does that do? As before stated, emotion, as the word indicates, is the "moving force" in man, the stream that makes the engine go. We may look on the mind as the form-builder, the creator of the intricate mechanism of achievement, but emotion, desire, is the steam which drives the engine. Now some people can create beautiful engines but have little steam to make them go. Others have a superabundance of steam, jetting out at all places, but a faulty or ill-constructed engine. Where the two are well made and well controlled, and united to physical efforts as well, there is no power in heaven or earth that can say nay to the will of man, in time.

Desire is a magnetic force bringing to a man always his true heart's desire. The scriptures tell us that "He shall give thee the desires of thine heart" (*Ps.* 37). Some will not believe this. "Look how many things I have wished for and never got," they will say. If it is only a passing wish, a pale, anaemic force fading out almost as soon as it is created, then of course it will not reach fulfilment. But if it is a whole-hearted desire, so intense as to fill the whole man, so undeviating and steady that desire has become converted into *Will*, then it must surely come. Yes, we may be run over and our body killed before that consummation is reached. The death of the body has not killed the radiating will. It will act again with the birth of a new body, early in life, and many a friend will say: "What a fortunate young person! Why do not such opportunities come my way too?" Opportunities do not come to those who have not ardently desired in the past, for *Desire creates opportunity*. Even the final, great discovery of God comes as the result of a tremendous, whole-hearted desire. "Blessed are the pure in heart: for they shall see God"; and purity means "whole-heartedness", the whole of oneself without diversion or otherness, the wholeness of "Holiness", the "single eye" which enables our body to be "full of light".

Another variant of desire is love and hate. The two are the positive and negative poles of the same force, and both equally attract objects. We may take it as an aphorism that all that which we truly love we can never, in all Eternity, lose. The people we love, the causes we love, the things we love, will come back to us again and again on the long journey of the soul.

And so will the things we hate and fear. How well that truth is expressed by the Prophet Job: "The thing which I feared has come upon me." Have we not often noticed that people often catch the bodily ills of which they are most afraid. Someone will exclaim: "Do we have to meet our enemies and the people we dislike again?" I do not think many people have *real* enemies, but those who have will certainly come across them again and again. Instantaneous dislike is quite common, and is summed up in the familiar doggerel:

> I do not love you, Dr. Fell,
> The reason why I cannot tell;
> But this I know full well,
> I do not love you, Dr. Fell.

Why did the Christ tell us to " love our enemies ", to " forgive " unto seventy times seven? Because in that way the force can be re-polarized to love, and hatred will cease. Said the Lord Buddha: " Hatred ceaseth never by hatred, hatred ceaseth only by love."

This is the real meaning of " forgiveness ". Not a condescending attitude which virtually says: " I will forgive you, but I shall chalk it up against you inside all the same." The derivation of the word shows us what forgiveness really is. It means " forth-giving ", a spontaneous, undemanding, self-forgetting *shining forth* of love. Who can resist that? And a great enemy makes a good friend, once the power is re-polarized, since the force of hatred has now become the force of love. Thus he who has been forgiven much, loves much. Resentment and anger will never cease, life after life, until one " forgives " and the repulsion ceases.

Sometimes, but rarely, repulsion may create a family relationship. I once knew a mother and daughter who had deep underlying dislike of each other. Coming to know the truth of the above statement the daughter set out to win her mother. Before the old lady died her once greatly disliked daughter had become the " apple of her eye ".

Is it a person we are devoted to? We shall find him again. Is it a cause our whole heart is given to? We shall come back to work for it again. For love has never known defeat, and overcomes time and space.

The third strand of our thread of life is action, which creates our physical environment, and this also includes speech. All speech and all action have one of two inevitable effects. They either help, cheer, encourage the movement of life around us, or they detract from it, create confusion and unhappiness, put stumbling-blocks in the way of others, cause depression and discouragement. It begins the moment we wake up in the morning, and whichever it may be, it is a force sent out into the universe, which will inevitably, one day, somewhere, return to its creator, ourselves. All forces generated and inspired by a *personal* motive, must return to their creator. This is the Law. We have disturbed the equilibrium of Nature and it will be reinstated at the point where it was generated—ourselves. Watch what happens when we throw a pebble into the centre of a still pond. The ripples go out to the very edge of the pond, and then begin to come back again, towards the centre of disturbance.

Even a word does that. Once spoken, it cannot be recalled. For good or ill it has gone. "Oh! if I had only *thought* a minute," say so many people, "I would not have said that!" But it is said and cannot be called back. What must we do then? We can send another force after it which will cause it to break off at another angle, like a billiard ball sent against another one moving forward. Have we said something hurtful, injurious? At once say something kind and helpful, or seek forgiveness. Have we injured someone? Seek to do him a service. For, as an Adept once said, the best repentance is the resolve not to do it again.

For, this follows an unbreakable law—the Law of Spiritual Dynamics. Science tells us that action and reaction are equal and opposite. Apply this to psychological action. We have it expressed by the Great Teachers in the so-called Golden Rule. The Christ expressed it thus: "Whatsoever ye would that men should do to you, do ye even so to them: for this is the law and the prophets." The law which St. Paul again defined when he wrote: "Be not deceived; God [the Life Force] is not mocked: for whatsoever a man soweth, that shall he also reap," and learn by the reaping.

So if our words and actions in the past have helped, cheered, or comforted, help and cheer will flow back to us. If by them we have shown unhappiness and frustration, sorrow and loss will come back to us. Thus the heavenly surgeon by very sorrowful means cuts out the cancer of cruelty and selfishness from the souls of men.

Sometimes the results are long in coming. They appear in another Day of Life. And sometimes great invisible Intelligences keep them away from a man for many lives until he has grown stronger and the reactions instead of crushing him will make him as gold tried in the furnace. When a man is nearing the end of his soul's journey the tragedies from the past come upon him swiftly, that he may be freed of these debts to Nature and learn their lessons. Thus the good suffer, and the wicked seem to flourish like the green bay tree. But Life is utterly true, and no man can finally escape the result of his actions. His "sin" will find him out somewhere, somewhen. The "wicked" are often the ignorant, the undeveloped amongst us. Life does not ask of them too hard a lesson yet.

Perhaps we are helpful to someone and he seems ungrateful. Gratitude is a virtue which belongs to the evolved. The immature do not always possess it. Is a baby "grateful" for the incessant care of its mother? But say the scriptures: "Cast thy bread upon the waters: for thou shalt find it after many days." Many days are lives sometimes, and the returning force may be as an unexpected bolt from the olue when all hope seemed gone.

We must not make the mistake of picturing these returning forces as mere invisible powers. They come to us through other people and events. When the disciple Peter, in excess of zeal in defence of his Lord, cut off a soldier's ear, the Christ, healing the wound, said: "Put up again thy sword . . . for all they that take the sword shall perish with the sword." And then He added: "It must needs be that offences come [if men have generated their causes]; but woe to that man by *whom* the offence cometh." Other people and our surroundings are thus the unconscious agents of the Law which brings to every man that which he hath sown. We have the free will to choose which we will be the agents of a man's happy fortune or of his ill-fate.

But do not let us in understanding this fall into the fatalistic attitude of some people and exclaim that this is the man's fate, and leave him to it. *We* are part of his fate and we are there to aid. That is what we are there for. As *The Voice of the Silence* puts it: "Inaction in a deed of mercy becomes an action in a deadly sin."

But how, someone will ask, does it come about that a selfish, ignorant man has every luxury this world can give him and the scholar and the saint so little? Two things must be noted here. First, material good is not always spiritual richness. "A man's life," said the Christ, "consisteth not in the abundance of the things which he possesseth." Second, we must remember that causes bring results on their own plane of causation. A physical action brings a physical result. A good action may be done with a bad motive. For example, a man may give a large sum to a hospital to get his name in the papers or win a title. The good action, which relieved hundreds of people, will bring him comfortable surroundings in another life, but the selfish motive will make a hard, narrow character.

It is also possible that a man may do something inherently evil with a good, though mistaken, motive. It is just conceivable that some of the ancient inquisitors really thought they were saving men's souls when they tortured their bodies. Then they might be born with a deformed or diseased body, but a patient spirit.

Arguments are sometimes started as to which is the worst sin. According to some it would seem to be some infringement of the man-made sexual code. There love sanctifies and selfishness brutalizes. The truly worst sin in life is cruelty, because it is an offence against the

Law of the Universe which is Love. Happy is the man who at the end of life can look back and see that he has never really hurt either man or beast or flower. An Adept once wrote to a young disciple: "The greatest consolation in and the foremost duty of life, child, is not to give pain, and avoid causing suffering to man or beast."

What is a good environment? Is it to be born "with a silver spoon in one's mouth"? Not wealth, but good and loyal friends, understanding parents, are the real richness of life. It is said that a Mahârâni came to see the Lord Buddha. She wished to ask Him three questions. "Lord," she said, "tell me, how can I be sure that, first, I shall be born beautiful; second, that I shall be wealthy; and third, that I shall have many friends, in my next life?" I heard this story many years ago in India, and I cannot now remember the Lord's answer to the first two questions. (I think material wealth is often the result of great desire for it in the past. I once knew a millionaire who told me that when he was only a little errand-boy, earning four shillings and six pence a week, he *knew* he would one day be wealthy. Evidently, the intention had come over from another life.) But the Lord's answer to the third question was as follows: "O Queen," He said, "if you would have many friends, then learn in this life to give away with both hands." The Blessed One's answer was the same as the Lord Christ's, when He advised men to give "good measure, pressed down and shaken together, and running over. . . . For with the same measure that ye mete withal it shall be measured to you again." The selfish, calculating spirit which says: "What am I getting out of this?" never yet won friends.

We may sum up the action of the threefold cord of Fate, then, in three aphorisms, first formulated by Dr. Annie Besant:

> Thought creates character and capacity;
> Desire brings us our opportunities;
> Action creates our environment.

CHAPTER VIII

THOUGHT—THE CREATOR

LET us consider what thought is and how it works, for it is the most powerful factor in our being either for good or for ill. The control and purification of the mind leads to the states above and beyond it, but if it becomes the master and not the servant of the man, and highly accentuated, it can shut the door upon heavenly verities. As *The Voice of the Silence* puts it: "The mind is the great slayer of the Real."

As before stated, thought is a vibration, a wave-length in the higher, subtler reaches of the soul or psychic body, which when we are "awake" immediately communicates itself to the interacting brain-cells, causing them to vibrate synchronously, but at a lower octave, so to say. The wave-lengths do not cease there, but communicate themselves also to the surrounding psychic atmosphere. Sensitive people are aware of this. They can dimly sense what another person is thinking and feeling, though he is silent and says nothing. But what do these sensitive thought-currents *do*, since it is idle to suppose they do nothing in particular?

Let us look at the question from two standpoints: first, what our thinking does to ourselves, and secondly, what it does to those around us.

To ourselves directly, it actually creates conditions and transforms us, making us what we are at any given moment. A man *is* the product of his thought. The scriptures tell us that. Says *Proverbs* that as a man "thinketh in his heart, so is he". We may in these modern days translate heart" as the subconscious, the whole content of past thinkings, not only of this life, but of previous lives also. Our whole outlook on life is coloured by our habitual thought, as someone looking out of a window through a coloured pane of glass sees a world thus conditioned. No one sees life exactly as it is, unless he has become absolutely impersonal, desireless and pure. We see life distorted by our prejudices, wishful thinkings, deep-seated desires. The sooner we recognize this fact, the more tolerant and humble we shall quickly become.

Trace a type of thought and see where it goes; and this will include a certain type of accompanying feeling, for very few people can think unaffected by feeling. First of all, it sets into motion the living, rapidly vibrating psychic self or soul. Psychic matter, like physical matter, easily acquires an habitual tendency to vibrate in a certain way. It may be that the thought-feeling was first evoked by some person or event outside. It tends to repeat itself. This finally establishes a groove or tendency in the mental self, and when firmly established becomes a permanent trait of character. For example, suppose some untoward event causes a tragic and gloomy outlook upon life. Life seems hard, cruel, inimical. If this thought be dwelt upon continuously it becomes an established thought-habit, making its thinker into a pessimist, who blames life and everybody for his misfortunes. The permanent trait of character influences action, which in turn creates destiny.

Can a trait of character be altered or uprooted? Yes, it can, by patient persistence in right thinking. As a trait becomes established by a certain type of thought, so an opposite type of thought, patiently persisted in, will gradually change and transform its wave-length. This is where the particular creative power of the imagination comes into play. " What! only the imagination," some people will exclaim. Consider the word " imagination ". It means the image-making faculty. Every thought pictured by the mind is at once actually created in the plastic matter of the surrounding mental world. If not thought of again it fades away, but if continually re-thought it acquires a certain consistency and hovers, held by magnetic attraction, in the vicinity of its creator, reacting upon him and his environment. Such permanent reacting thought-forms sometimes become what psychologists call deep-seated " complexes ". A long-held " grudge " is of this type. Such a thought-form acquires a dim elemental life, which has a dim feeling of self-preservation. It does not *want* to fade out, so, if we can picture a thought-form thinking, it urges its creator: " Think me again so that I may go on living!" This is the true origin of what are called "tempting devils". When a man is trying to get over a bad habit, say drink, his strongly reacting thought-forms suggest the satisfaction of his craving, but he has created these tempters himself. It is very hard to refuse to listen to them; but if a man will do it and endure the pain of craving until the "tempters" die out, it will trouble him no more.

Our mind is like a lantern shining upon the path of life, enabling us to "see". Some have brighter and better lamps than others, but it is always enough for us to see the next step. When we cast the light of that lantern down the road of life up which we have ascended, the past, we see pictures from that past, memories. Generally the most vivid "memories" are those which have a strong emotional content, or contain a problem as yet unsolved. Happy is he who has only beautiful memories, memories of lovely or heroic acts, seen or shared; not ugly memories of injuries and slights. This is part of what the Lord Buddha called Right Memory in His Noble Eightfold Path.

When we cast the light of our minds forward, up the road of life before us, the future, we see pictures of hopes, ideals, wishes, and sometimes momentary shining intimations of immortality. These are not "just imaginary"; they are real things, thought-forces created by our own needs and aspirations. They represent what we *shall be*. For here is an interesting fact: no one can picture thus anything which is not germane to his own deepest nature. With a kind of divine clairvoyance we thus see what we have the innate power to become, in time.

We may call the past, its whole content, both of this life and all previous lives, the *sub*-conscious; and the whole future, with its illimitable, mounting vistas of beauty and joy, may be called our *super*-consciousness. The more evolved a man is, the longer he has lived in the great School of Life, the more potent is the growing effect of the superconscious Self. Dr. Volgyesi, a prominent Hungarian psycho-analyst, has discovered this. He claims that, with his more cultured and sensitive patients, he has found it far more effective to get them in tune with their higher selves than to dig about in the debris of their lower, past selves, where now it is better to let " sleeping dogs lie ". He also states that some form of meditation or yoga is a necessity for the modern man.

I think this is the true meaning of the parable of the Christ where He said to the man full of excuses: " Follow me; and let the dead bury their dead." Let the dead past bury the dead past. So many of us walk along the road of life with our heads turned over our shoulders, peering continually into the past. Is it any wonder that we continually stumble and trip up? It is far more important to look ahead where you are going for there " the Christ in you, the hope of glory" lifted up like a far-away star, is drawing you continually nearer to Himself. *Light on the Path* calls it the " dim star that burns within," and says that " steadily, as you watch and worship, its light will grow stronger"; and that one day "its light will suddenly become the Infinite Light". There we see pictured the man of God's intending and man's aspiring.

But suppose we let the light of our minds shine steadily on the spot where for a moment we are standing —clearly, steadily, unstrained. This is "concentration". The fruit of it is inspiration and understanding. We must *wait* for that to come. Most people have no patience to "wait". They want an answer to all their problems *at once*. A very deep form of concentration comes to the man trained by long years of quiet thought and life; it is called "contemplation" in which a man's unveiled spiritual perception comes face to face with That Which Is. Says the Psalmist: "I waited patiently for the Lord; and he inclined unto me, and heard my cry." But would that have happened had he not "waited"? It may be that the object of our still thought is an ideal to be achieved, a problem to be solved, a person to be understood. Let the light of thought rest quietly, unconstrainedly, without prior conclusions, upon the subject of our thinking, and presently, from the darkness, flashes of insight, inspiration, intimations will break in, because we have waited and hoped and prayed, and not claimed them.

Characters can thus be altered. There are occasions when we all wish we were a little better and nicer than we are. We sometimes make half-hearted resolutions, say on New Year's Eve, soon to be forgotten. Often we lay the blame (a foolish proceeding anyhow) for what we are on heredity, our upbringing, the State, life, anything, in fact, but where it really belongs—ourselves. Because most men do not understand life, they often leave it little better in development than they came in with. We *could* leave it very different indeed, if only we knew how to put our own wills and intelligence beside the gentle pressure of the Great Evolutionary Will. To build a character is something like building a house. First, the architect makes a plan, a blue-print, but the house cannot be built more quickly than one brick at a time. The mind and imagination are the architects. Numerous actions founded on their plan are the bricks.

Before we begin to build, let us take honest stock of ourselves, of our assets and liabilities of character. Many psychological schools advise us to do this. One business school says: " Find out your weakest spot, for it will always be letting you down in life, and if you do not know it, ask all your friends for they will be sure to know it! " Having decided what it is—bad temper, lack of perseverance, anything—do not dwell on it ineffectually, for that lends it added power by our thought, but begin to picture its opposite excellence. Inquire what it is, how it works, how it manifests quite naturally in someone who has it (but did not always possess it in the past). Then picture circumstances likely to occur in one's own life where one will be tried in this respect, and imagine oneself acting in the desired manner. This must be done for a few minutes every day, but do not be surprised if it is quite a time before it begins to affect action. Many times will we forget and say: " There now! I intended to do quite differently." We have to weigh the scales slowly till they tip in the other direction; or, to quote William James, let us create a " new pathway of neural discharge ".

But time and perseverance will do it. There will come a day when we shall remember in time, and then we may be conscious of two contrary forces: on the one hand, the old habit straining at the leash to go ahead, and, on the other hand, the newly formed resolution. When the moment comes that we really *do* act in the new way, we shall be already rewarded, for a sense of power will flood our whole being. This is the secret of the " poise " so much talked of by psychologists. Poise is nothing more than the certainty that we can deal with ourselves, not other people. " Greater is he," said the Buddha, " who conquers himself than he who takes ten cities."

A famous example of this kind of procedure was Benjamin Franklin. He aimed at becoming a perfect character, and to facilitate this task, wrote down twelve leading characteristics which he endeavoured to practise, a week each in rotation. At night when he wrote his diary he would note where he had failed and record it by a black spot therein. " I am glad to say," he writes, " that after a time the black spots grew less." That meant, of course, that he was acquiring the new habit. His twelve virtues form a rather quaint list to the ears of modern man. " Orderliness " was one, and he confesses that this one he never really achieved. He mentioned his practice to a Quaker friend, who commented: "Methinks, Benjamin, that thou lackest humility." Franklin decided he was right and added humility to the list. He writes later on: "I have had great success with the appearance of this virtue, but not, alas! with the reality of it." Perhaps he thought humility was talking like Uriah Heep, whereas the best description I ever heard was this: "Humility does not consist in belittling ourselves (this is often inverted pride). It consists in not thinking about ourselves at all."

An interesting fact in Nature is that every virtue evolves out of a vice, and every virtue is indissolubly connected with others, so that to achieve one is at the same time to acquire others. H. P. Blavatsky tells us that all virtues are founded on the recognition of the One Life. In fact we may put it this way, that all virtues are the result of pure self-forgetting, self-annihilating devotion to the good and happiness of others, to that true unselfishness which is pure love. Conversely, the root of all "sin" is selfishness, working for the little separated self alone, calculating only what *it* is getting out of things, without consideration for the welfare of all others.

One thing here is to be guarded against. The development of virtues must not be allowed to accentuate the sense of "I"; otherwise it may become a dangerous practice. We must never become complacent, smug, never feel satisfied that *we* are strong, wise, unselfish, etc. We must aim only at striving to channel better the love-power of the universe, that we may add to the sum total of happiness in this world, and "try to lift a little of the heavy karma of the world"; that we may give our small aid "to the few strong hands that hold back the powers of darkness from obtaining completely victory".

Not only in the realm of character-building can we use and develop our thought-power. Some people will say that they have "no brains". Now nearly every one has enough brains to get along with. The trouble is that most people do not use them to anything like their full capacity, or develop them in any way. Did we not go to school, they will say, and have a good education? School and college may give us a great mass of information. They do not always teach *how to think*, and it is by our own native, unhindered thinking that our intelligence develops. Intelligence is *not* intellectualism. In fact, too much intellectuality may kill a native intelligence. Here, again, as in the higher reaches of our being, "the mind is the great slayer of the Real".

Thought-power is developed by only one thing—*by thinking*. Do we not all think? Do we not all read a great deal—read the newspapers through, for example? Reading what other people say, without thinking about it ourselves, is often a drugging of the mind, an escape from thought. I do not suggest that we become too serious about this, and *never* read for pleasure and relaxation. Lewis Carrol, the author of *Alice in Wonderland*, once wrote an amusing but wise little book called *Feeding the Mind*. He said that feeding the mind was an analogous process to feeding the stomach. What would happen if we gave our stomachs a continual diet of jam-puffs and snippets, and never any real digestible food? An enervated and weakened system would soon become evident. Not only must we provide it with suitable food, but we must not take too much, especially at once, " gulping it down " as the saying is. We should masticate it well before swallowing. Much irritation and nervousness are the result of a " starved mind ".

Apply these principles to the mind. Every day we should give it a little, easily digested, real food, and we should masticate it well; in the words of a Church of England collect, we should " read, mark, learn, and inwardly digest ". In other words, read a little every day of some book you like which has real thought, but not too quickly. Stop at the end of a sentence which contains an idea or statement, and think it well over. See what *you* think about it. This means slow reading. It may be a little tiresome to him who has never done it. He may stop to think and find that no thoughts come. He needs to persevere; after a time, ideas, inspirations, understanding will begin to flash in. Stop again at the close of a paragraph and sum up its message, its gist, in a few words of your own. Write it down, if desired. We may even do this with a whole chapter, or even with the whole book. It steadies and deepens the mind, and the method of summation develops another quality, the ability to see the essentials not only in a book but also in life itself.

But the mind needs also to be widened as well as deepened. Here we must beware of developing prejudices and complexes, for they will entirely close the mind and prevent it expanding in certain directions, as also will fanaticism on any point. It is well to try impartially and sympathetically to estimate another point of view, even one violently opposed to our own. Let us not read papers and articles only of our own brand of thinking. Let us not think only about that which is stated in books. Their only value lies in the truth or otherwise in what they say about life. Why not go sometimes directly to life itself? Let us try to understand life, understand others, understand ourselves who have exactly the same reactions as all others, by deep thought, observation and inquiry. For "Life itself has speech," says *Light on the Path*, "and is never silent." And it asks us to regard earnestly all the life that surrounds us: "Learn to look intelligently into the hearts of men. . . . Study the hearts of men, that you may know what is that world in which you live. . . . Regard the constantly changing and moving life which surrounds you, for it is *formed by the hearts of men*; and as you learn to understand their constitution and meaning, you will by degrees be able to read the larger word of life."

Only one thing is more difficult to know, says this ancient scripture, and that is our own heart. These things can only be clearly discerned from an impersonal viewpoint, and it is so difficult to be truly impersonal about ourselves. Yet through our own heart comes the one light which can illuminate life, and make it clear to our eyes. A Master of the Wisdom once wrote to a disciple: "Learn to look on yourself with the calmness of an utter stranger, and do not be led into either anxiety or remorse." Remorse is a continual leakage of psychic force towards a regretted action in the past; anxiety is a similar leakage towards a feared event in the future which may never happen. "Live in the eternal," from moment to moment, trusting all to Life, as a bird trusts itself to the air, undoubtingly. Have we erred? Should we have learnt wisdom without erring? Do we fear the future? We need never cross a bridge before it comes. The root of remorse and fear is the little, personal self. The divine Self knows no such things. It has the deathless courage of its own immortality.

Many schools of religious thought enjoin a daily self-examination upon their devotees. This is a good way to get to know oneself if one does not get too wrapped up in it, too self-conscious. A virtue or a service of which one is self-conscious is neither a virtue nor a service. The soul must be unfettered, the desires free, spontaneous. And they become this when a man no longer thinks "*I* am" this or the other great or beautiful thing, but realizes that "only God is great, that all good work is done by God alone". Let us look on our abilities and qualities of character as a workman looks on his tools. He does not think he *is* his tools. If he has leisure he sharpens and mends them. If he has not, he does the best he can with them.

Now let us consider the effect our thinking has upon our surroundings. Of course the general effect we have upon our surroundings consists in the steady radiation of what we habitually *are*. This is the unspoken gift of each one of us to the world, far more important than what we say, or even do. "What you are," wrote Ralph Waldo Emerson, "speaks so loudly to me that I cannot hear what you say." A strong and noble character is as a tree in a thirsty land where others seek shelter.

But when we think specifically about anything, something special occurs. We may lay it down as an axiom that *whatever* we think of, in heaven above, or on earth beneath, *that* we are at once in touch with, and by that very thought a magnetic *rapport* is established immediately. Thought annihilates time and space.

Suppose we think of a friend of ours. He may be on the other side of the world, but as we think of him we contact him, and if he is very sensitive it may cause him to think of us. Have we not sometimes had the experience of finding the thought of a friend continually recurring during the day and perhaps the next day receiving a letter from him?

This is equally true when someone we love passes beyond the veil. He is not out of reach of our thoughts. Nay, he is even more sensitive to them, for he is now dwelling in a world where thought-forces are very potent. There was once a man who was an invalid and bed-ridden for many years, but he was a very beautiful character and many people loved him. After his death he carried over the thought-habit of being very tired and so he was allowed to "rest", and it seemed to him that wonderful influences of comfort surrounded him. These were formed by the loving thoughts of his friends left behind. Can we pray for the dead? Why not, since a prayer is only a consecrated thought?

There is no force in the world more powerful than loving thought. It can prove a veritable shield to the loved one thought of. Perhaps people will never know what they owe to the loving thoughts and prayers of those who remember them. A loving thought is a gift, a gift from our very souls. It springs from our souls, flies to the object of our thought, and when he is responsive becomes part of him. To love and be loved is an exchange between souls. We may be too poor to send a gift of money, but how much more beautiful to send our love which never fails to reach its object.

Sometimes we give our trust and our belief. Many a man has been saved by a friend who believed in him even when he had lost faith in himself. What lovely things we can give to people! Why do we give them unlovely things sometimes? Unlovely thoughts create real forces too, and they reach the person thus thought of and act on him as a discouraging, devitalizing power. Sometimes we have to live beside a person who has no faith whatever in our ability to do anything well. How hard then it becomes to try! Inwardly we must take up arms against a sea of such unseen troubles. In family life there is a good deal of this kind of mental cruelty. Especially is it the case with children whose plastic inner selves reflects so easily the moods and opinions of those around them. Malicious gossip too, deluging someone with unhelpful and untrue thought-forces, is actually cruel. What can we do if we happen to be the victim of such remarks? We must not think them back, but try to return good thoughts for evil, and then the unhelpful forces will find no harbourage, and may even return to the senders. This is how curses are said to come home to roost.

We can develop the power which we exercise unconsciously—of sending thoughts. We can regularly think with love of those we love or desire to aid. To help those who are ill, tired or discouraged, sit down quietly and picture them, not as ill or tired or sad but with light and happiness glowing and shining round them. *Think* of them with thoughts of help, encouragement and blessing. This can also be done by a group of friends all thinking together. Think thoughts too of the nation, and of the world, hoping always the best for all.

Yet one other way there is in which our thought influences our environment. Houses and buildings where people think many similar thoughts become in time deeply impregnated with them. This can be sensed and read by an experienced psychometrist. But we all know it to some extent. Do we not feel, when we enter a house, whether here reign love and peace or bickering and enmity? Religious buildings are saturated with religious thought and aspiration. The "atmosphere" of a home is far more important than its furnishings and appurtenances. Even a town has an atmosphere, a psychology of its own, and a country even more so.

Thought is truly a tremendous power, as scheming politicians have discovered in these days, with their calculated use of mass propaganda.

Long years ago an Adept said: "Ideas rule the world, and as men's minds receive new ideas the world will advance, mighty revolutions will spring from them." Here are some more words from the same Master of the Wisdom: "For countless generations hath the Adept builded a fane of imperishable rocks, a giant's tower of INFINITE THOUGHT, emerging at the end of every cycle, to invite the elect of mankind to co-operate with him and help in his turn enlighten superstitious man."

As before stated, not intelligence but intellectuality alone can work evil. H. P. Blavatsky says that the mind, unillumined by the spiritual nature, is the veritable devil in man. It can be and often is the "slayer of the Real". That aspect of man is being predominatingly developed just now. Intellectual pursuit and discovery have outstripped spiritual growth. There lies a great danger today. Another Adept shortly expressed it thus: "At this point the world teems with the results of intellectual activity and spiritual decrease." To paraphrase a familiar proverb we may say that "the mind alone is a good servant but a bad master".

There is the consecrated use of thought and emotion in prayer and meditation. It is all summed up in the familiar words of St. Paul:

> Finally, brethren, whatsoever things are true, whatsoever things are honest, whatsoever things are just, whatsoever things are pure, whatsoever things are lovely, whatsoever things are of good report; if there be any virtue, and if there be any praise, think on these things.

CHAPTER IX

LOVE—THE HEALER

LET us remember that the word " emotion " means the " moving force ". Without feeling life has no joy, no thrill, no real meaning. One finds so many people whose emotions have become rather arid. They come to me and say: " I don't believe I love anyone in this world." Being human they have the capacity to do so, but emotion, like thought and the physical muscles, must be *used* to grow and develop, otherwise it will tend to atrophy.

Let us ask ourselves: " Do we love, really love, or do we only seek to *be* loved ? " For to love is the life-breath of our souls, and the man who does not love is already dead. As has been already stated, perhaps that is the chief lesson life would teach us, *how to love*. " What! " some people will exclaim, " everybody knows how to love, it is natural to all." No, to love truly is *not* entirely natural. In many a case it has to be learnt. That which passes for love is a pale, anaemic shadow of true love, and with many it is nothing more than self-love projected upon someone else. The " love " which keeps a son or daughter waiting hand and foot upon one until the years steal their youth and capacity for joy is not love but self-love. Nor is the jealous watchfulness of a husband or wife a proof of love, only of pride and self-regard. Even "mother-love" is not always true love. Sometimes it is an expression of a sense of personal possession and pride, and the unfortunate victim of it is not infrequently psychically smothered.

Then what is true love? The above examples show us what it is *not*, and also indicate the root of the trouble, the personal equation. Perfect love makes no demands, imposes no obligations, never tries to improve or criticize, hopes always for the best, is faithful and unchanging no matter what happens, and therefore is a saving, redeeming force. It has been well described in a Tibetan scripture that there are seven forms of love, three of which belong to men and four to the Gods. The most primitive form is sheer magnetic attraction, such as, in another form, keeps atoms and molecules together, and planets and systems revolving in their due order. Between two bodies this urge ceases on fulfilment, as the electricity disappears when the positive and negative poles of two magnetized needles meet. This surface attraction is often mistaken for love. People get married on it and wake to find themselves wedded to a stranger. What must they do then? Get to know the stranger; no marriage will endure where preliminary attraction has not developed into an enduring friendship. Quite often a passing friendship is formed by this magnetic power, but easily broken and dissolved at the first serious difference.

A higher form, says the scripture, is what we might call psychic, and is on a reciprocal, *tu quoque* basis. "I will love you if you will love me, and remember you owe me something for loving you." This, it is said, carries within it the seeds of its own death.

The third form approaches the ways of Gods and is a little difficult for man, and so generally has to be learnt. It is so to love our beloved ones that we desire only their highest good, and on their own terms, not ours. I remember a woman telling me that she had dropped a friend because that friend did not come up to the ideal she had formed of her. What impertinence! It is surely enough if the friend approximates to her own ideal. True love does not make ideals of what other people ought to be, does not try to improve them, alter them, correct them. It may be the duty of parents and teachers to correct a child sometimes, and even then with due understanding of that soul's make-up and tendencies, but it is not always the duty of a friend to correct and improve another. So often the true motive is not that this is "for their own good", but the conscious or unconscious spirit of domination.

True love is for ever faithful, eternally loyal. In Shakespeare's words: "Love is not love which alters when it alteration finds," because it is making no demands, asking nothing back.

The most wonderful description of love is contained in the thirteenth chapter of *I Corinthians*. There it is called "charity". But what is charity? It is not giving a needy person something that possibly we do not want ourselves. The derivation of the word shows us what it is. It comes from the Latin, *carus*, dear. The charitable man is the one to whom all things are dear. Henry Drummond calls it the Spectrum of Love, the seven qualities enumerated by St. Paul being like the seven colours which appear when a white ray of light is passed through a prism. It will not be out of place to enumerate them again here.

"Love suffereth long, and is kind"; this is the patience and kindness of true love.

"Love envieth not"; it is too unselfish and generous to envy or be jealous. A friend's success is our success; his sorrow is ours. If we are secretly envious of a friend's success we do not truly love him. Our love for him has been rendered impure by our own self-love.

"Love vaunteth not itself, is not puffed up"; this is the humility of love, which does not consider that it is somebody and therefore in a position to make claims on others.

"Doth not behave itself unseemly"; love is truly courteous. This is the root of being a gentleman; it means a delicate and scrupulous consideration for the rights and feelings of all others. When courtesy flies out of the home, disharmony and unhappiness come in. Familiarity must never breed in a husband or a wife contempt for the life-partner, and even a little child should be treated with respect and consideration if love would reign.

"Seeketh not her own"; the unselfishness of love. Another's good, another's happiness is her paramount concern, never her own. "Is not easily provoked"; love is of a peaceful and generous temper.

"Thinketh no evil"; there is a beautiful, guileless simplicity about real love. It is so slow to think the worst, so eager to think the best. It "rejoiceth not in iniquity"; does not find pleasure in evil-speaking and gossip. These are so often the signs of a poor, starved heart, not of one rich in love.

"Beareth all things, believeth all things"—let us say believeth *in* all things according to their deepest nature; "hopeth all things, endureth all things"; "Love never faileth"; is thus undefeatedly loyal.

It is far, far more important to love than to be loved, though the ability to love often begins in infancy when a child is truly loved. Doctors and psychologists have discovered that juvenile delinquency, criminal tendencies and over-sexual proclivities take their rise from an unloved and insecure childhood. Many a man or woman who suffers from perverted or over-sexed proclivities is really love-starved. Children will learn to love by being loved. We can teach our children no better thing in life.

The destroyer of love is too much self and selfishness. To claim, to demand, to consider a right, to impose our ideas or will upon another, is to put an end to love. A life-convinct, writing under the name of Starr Daily, found this out in prison. His first book, *Love*

Can Open Prison Doors, swept the world. Here is a good extract from his book, *Release*:

> There is a selfish emotion that hurts. It has often been called love. It is but a shadow of the miracle-worker. . . . Just as science, art and invention do not desire to reform anybody, neither does love. By not wanting to reform others it transforms them. By setting others free, love binds them. A friend is a lover. He does not preach, find fault, condemn. He frees; and the things he frees, he binds. You cannot have the thing you will not give away. You cannot be free of a thing you hold. To hold on is to belong to the thing held, a *bond*. What you set free belongs to you. You do not belong to it, for you belong to love. . . . All things below love encircle and squeeze. They press and inflict and hurt. Love is Reality, the liberator, the miracle-worker. By making others glad, you give them a foretaste of heaven on earth.

The poet, artist and mystic, William Blake, said the same thing:

> He who bends to himself a Joy
> Doth the winged life destroy;
> Who kisses the Joy as it flies
> Lives in Eternity's sunrise.

Of all the many motive forces in life, there are fundamentally only Love and Hate, and all others are derivatives from these two; those which spring from Love are creative, constructive, healing, life-giving. Those which arise from Hate are mutually destructive, hurtful, death-dealing. Some of the derivatives of love are appreciation, encouragement, admiration, sympathy and trust. We actually live and grow by these, especially children. This truth was beautifully voiced by Wordsworth:

> We live by admiration, hope and love,
> And even as these are well and wisely fixed,
> In dignity of being we ascend.

In his famous *Ode on . . . Intimations of Immortality*, he writes:

> Shades of the prison-house begin to close
> Upon the growing boy,
> But he beholds the light, and whence it flows,
> He sees it in his joy.

Then how cruel to dim, darken or destroy the " vision splendid " by which all youth is attended.

The spirit of competition is wrong in our schools, and in life in general. We should be glad when others succeed, admire and bless them, not reach out to grab prestige, honour, success, love for ourselves.

The derivatives of Hate include harsh criticism, imputing of evil motives, slander and easy suspicion. They may be milder than murder, but they are of the same nature, death-dealing, creators of misery and shame. Quite truly did the Christ say that the man who hated his brother without a cause (purely personal jealousy being no real cause) was guilty in a lesser degree of the crime of murder. The desire and intent to hurt is the same. If resentment against a deadly injury is nursed and vengeance sought, the oscillations of hate and injury can continue for many lives. So let us love, appreciate, encourage. It is not our business to seek vengeance or retaliation.

"Vengeance is mine, saith the Lord"; which means that the great Law of Spiritual Dynamics will adjust all hurts done to others, impersonally and therefore justly, curatively, and will not be vindicative, as so often human "justice" is.

"Beloved," wrote the beloved disciple John, "let us love one another: for love is of God; and everyone that loveth is born of God, and knoweth God."

Dr. George Arundale once wrote that "Friendship is more to be cherished than psychic powers, than knowledge, than erudition, than oratory, than any power of mind, emotion or body, as our First Object points out."

Pure love, divine will-to-good, is a healing force. Doctors or nurses who love their patients are real healers, and even "miracles" will happen sometimes by their simple love and patience and prayer.

No wonder that the ancient Romans said: *Omnia vincit amor*! "Love conquers all."

CHAPTER X

LIFE—THE TEACHER

BY now it must be clear that life is a great School for the soul, and that the events of life as they follow each other are the teachers in that School; patient, firm, undeviating are these teachers, yet essentially loving in the truest sense of the term, because always bringing us nearer to our highest good. So many of us are like careless, uncomprehending children, knowing little of that deep purpose, and therefore not seeking to co-operate with it. Yet we do realize that the wisest and most compassionate amongst us are those who have pondered on and learnt of life, not only of books and theories.

As before described, it is our speech and actions that finally create our environment and the events of life. Nothing can come to us which does not belong to us. If in the liquidation of " group karma " we suffer over-much, a corresponding compensation becomes ours. The laws of the universe, outer and inner, are absolutely just. There is no favouritism, and they cannot be placated, turned aside, or prevented from acting by any means whatever. God is Justice, vast, implacable, im-personal justice. But He is also Mercy, because every just result of our thought, speech and deeds, however tragic-seeming, is not a vengeful but a curative force. It seems as if a heavenly surgeon cuts away a diseased aspect of the soul, for instance, in persons with the vice of cruelty—the most provocative among all sins of tragic results. Such sorrow, such loss, such pain, awaits the cruel man, but it is the only way by which that selfish obtuseness can be extirpated from his soul.

Nature's Laws do not act upon a " tit-for-tat " basis; i.e. I kill you in one life so you kill me in another. At any moment in time a myriad of forces is converging towards some one particular event. It looms in the astral light before it precipitates here, and may even be glimpsed prophetically in a dream or vision. But such a looming result is never truly fixed. At any moment a new factor may be introduced by the coming recipient, causing it to materialize rather differently. Hence it is always wise to be optimistic and to meet each event in a courageous spirit.

In what way should we face life's trials and tribulations, its events happy and unhappy, its success or failure, gain or loss? First, let us realize that what comes to us is truly ours, rightfully and gainfully belongs to us, no matter what it be. This will make for a contented spirit and cure us of the paralyzing vice of self-pity. The occultist is never sorry for himself and therefore he has the time and energy to be sorry for other people. Let us also remember that every reaction of life, whatever it may be, is for our ultimate good. It is a " lesson ", sometimes dark and mysterious, but through it the Voice of God is speaking to our souls. An old mystic, the Abbé de Caussarde, wrote that God still speaks to men as of old, through prophets and mystics, but most of all through the events of life. He speaks to every man through the little events of daily life, and to nations through the great world events. The great Saints have always felt that, even when events were tragic and painful. Does a word or a deed of another "hurt" us? Do not let us give way to resentment, revenge or self-pity. There is one thing always to be remembered: it could not hurt us were there not an element of truth in it. An accusation, wildly improbable and untrue, may amuse but never hurt. Our very frank friends who tell us what they think of us sometimes hold a mirror to our souls whereby we may glimpse a fact hitherto hidden to us.

Let us sit down quietly and realize these three things —that no event in life is unjust, but somewhere from the long past our ancient "sin" has found us out; that every event is remedial; and that it has a message, a lesson for us. It is designed to help us gain the tremendous knowledge of ourselves; to teach us that it is only on stepping-stones of dead and understood past selves that we continually rise to higher things, that this process has been going on for lives and will be going on for lives yet. This should produce humility in ourselves and tolerance and mercy towards others; also a deathless courage. As a Master of the Wisdom once put it, courage belongs to the immortal soul. The mortal body knows only the law of self-preservation. Courage is the red badge of our immortal Spirit, who lives and grows by sacrifice and faith and love.

Sorrow comes to all men " as the sparks fly upward ", which means as the divine Self ascends. It is the common lot of man. So often we think that our own sorrow is greater than anyone else's, but it is rarely true. Always there is someone who has yet a heavier burden to carry.

Sorrow is generally the result of loss. The pain which comes with sorrow is the pain of loss. But what heaven takes with one hand it gives again with another hand in another way. Emerson calls this the Law of Compensation. The loss of someone dearly loved, ah! what agony of spirit is ours. What causes it? The tremendous sense of loss. No longer have we the comfort and the joy of a dear and familiar presence. But be comforted, my friends, it is only an apparent loss. We can never lose that which we truly love. And the temporary loss tends to teach us to love on a higher level, tends to kill a sense of personal possession. Dr. Annie Besant once said to the writer: " When you can be just as happy when the one you love best is not here, you have learnt how to love."

The failure, the frustration of hopes and ambitions —how hard are these to bear. Yet the brave man, wrote Kipling, stoops to build again with " worn out tools ". " Ambition," says *Light on the Path*, " is the first curse. . . . Its results turn to dust and ashes . . . it shows the man at last that to work for self is to work for disappointment." That same scripture tells us to "desire power ardently", but to hunger for that which can be shared by every one and thus "to accumulate wealth for that united spirit of life which is our only true Self". If we have that spirit, no failure will daunt us, no disappointment really hurt us. We shall have the spirit which inspired Annie Besant's life and which she so well voiced in an address to Indian youth:

> Never forget that Life can only be nobly inspired and rightly lived if you take it bravely and gallantly, as a splendid adventure in which you are setting out into an unknown country, to face many a danger, to meet many a joy, to find many a comrade, to win and lose many a battle.

Suppose that ill-health overtakes us and thus limits our joy in life and power to do many things. This may well be used to turn inwards towards more immortal realms. I once knew a woman of splendid physique, whose chief aim in life seemed to be horses and hunting. One day a bad accident in the hunting field condemned her for the rest of her life to a couch. She said to me: "I was always a fine body, thinking of nothing but physical activity. Now I am beginning to be a soul."

Have we lost many opportunities, perhaps through native weakness of character? Other opportunities will come. The pain of lost opportunities is always a selfish one—what *we* have missed. We may in the future try to have bigger, more unselfish motives, and cultivate more power to rule and conquer our lazy, procrastinating selves!

Do people seem to misunderstand us often, ascribe to us mean motives we do not possess? Perhaps we possessed and hid them in the past and the vice of past hypocrisy is now bearing fruit. The true occultist must arrive at a point where the opinions of others affect him not, unless it may be to serve as pointers towards deeper self-discovery. An Eastern text says: "Regret nothing: fear nothing: but cut all doubts with the sword of knowledge."

But what about the awful pain of conscious shame and guilt? What a terrible lesson from Life, but perhaps it may teach us humility and selflessness. Why should we not suffer shame as well as others? Does it not add honesty and integrity to our souls to be "found out"? "Remember," says *Light on the Path*, "that the sin and shame of the world are your sin and shame." And "the vices of men become steps in the ladder, one by one, as they are surmounted. . . . Do not condemn the man that yields; stretch out your hand to him as a brother pilgrim whose feet have become heavy with mire." All pain is so hard to bear, but Edward Carpenter said: "Every pain that I suffered in one body became a power that I wielded in the next."

Perhaps worse than our own suffering is to watch another suffer. How willingly would we take that burden upon our own shoulders if we might. But Life, which is God, is wiser than we are. We cannot take the trouble away, but we can halve it by sharing it, by standing in with the sufferer. Say the scriptures: " None of them can by any means redeem his brother, nor give to God a ransom for him." Let us with heartfelt sympathy help our brothers to learn and not to evade the lessons of life. H. P. Blavatsky once wrote:

> As soon as he begins to understand what a friend and teacher pain can be, the Theosophist stands appalled before the mysterious problem of human life, and though he may long to do good works, equally he dreads to do them wrongly until he has himself acquired greater power and knowledge. The ignorant doing of good works may be vitally injurious, as all but those who are blind in their love of benevolence are compelled to acknowledge.

She also wrote:

> Harmony is the law of life, discord its shadow, whence springs suffering, the teacher, the awakener of consciousness.
>
> Through joy and sorrow, pain and pleasure, the soul comes to a knowledge of itself; then begins the task of learning the laws of life, that the discords may be resolved, and the harmony restored.
>
> The eyes of wisdom are as the ocean depths; there is neither joy nor sorrow in them; therefore the soul of the occultist must be stronger than joy, and greater than sorrow.

There is no such tremendous teacher, so wonderful a teacher, as Life itself. Not only in its sorrowful aspects but in its delicate, lovely, joyous aspects too. Living in cities separates man quite largely from healthy, natural living. Happy is the child who grows up in loving touch with natural things, birds and beasts and plants; for every natural thing can be an Epiphany, an intimation of Divinity.

We who would like to hear the Voice of God can see Him in every lovely thing, can hear Him in all the common events of life. To a heart that is truly dedicated to the Eternal Heart of the Universe, there is nothing common or unclean, for every event and problem which comes before us is converse with that Great Heart.

And so the brave man is the humble and true man whose faith in Life and its increasing purpose is like that of the little bird who flies undoubtingly into the empyrean. Robert Browning voiced this in very beautiful words:

> One who never turned his back but marched breast
> forward,
> Never doubted clouds would break,
> Never dreamed, though right were worsted, wrong
> would triumph;
> Held, we fall to rise, are baffled to fight better,
> Sleep to wake.

CHAPTER XI

WHAT SHOULD WE DO?

ALL religions and all civilizations have ethical standards which have become more or less customary. These vary somewhat for different races and in different ages. But behind them all there are dim and sometimes distorted reflections of the true and eternal Laws of the Universe. These latter are the real "Commandments of God" and, as before stated, they not only rule the physical universe, but the psychic and spiritual worlds as well.

Here we come up against a universal question: What is "sin"; is there such a thing? Strictly speaking, there is not; there is only *lack of growth*. Very few people deliberately and consciously commit sin out of pure devilry. They are mostly driven by blind impulses which they neither understand nor can control. The Indian scriptures describe the "qualities" of matter in Nature as *gunas*, and depict the wise man as watching the play of human life as "the *gunas* move amid the *gunas*".

This does not mean that no man has any responsibility for what he does. The sense of responsibility grows with a man's soul-growth. H. P. Blavatsky says that a deep sense of responsibility is a sign of spiritual maturity. Only the evolved man knows well that he is his brother's keeper.

Dr. Hastings, in his *Dictionary of the Bible*, writes: "Three cognate forms in Hebrew with no distinction of meaning express sin as *missing one's aim*, and correspond to the Greek and its cognates in the New Testament. The etymology does not suggest a person against whom the sin is committed, and does not necessarily imply intentional wrong-doing. The form translated 'iniquity' literally means perversion or distortion, and indicates a quality of action rather than an act itself. Again in the New Testament, the two Greek words translated as sin presuppose the existence of a 'law'."

It is as if an archer shot at a target and through lack of skill went wide of the mark, a lack of what the *Bhagavad Gita* calls "skill in action". How could we acquire that skill except by repeated trial and error and by suffering the consequences of the error? Thus life teaches, pain teaches, just retribution teaches. A child is ignorant, but as he grows his ignorance lessens. A soul is ignorant, but as many lives pass that primeval ignorance slowly dissipates.

We are told that we all suffer from "original sin". Now, the most *original* thing in all of us is not sin, but Divinity. *Light on the Path* puts it quite beautifully:

> There is a natural melody, an obscure fount in every human heart. It may be hidden over and

> utterly concealed and silenced—but it is there. At the very base of your nature you will find faith, hope and love.

That which is original in all of us is original ignorance, or, as the Indian scriptures put it, *avidya*, "without the true knowledge". The Indian books also say that the root of all sin is the "heresy of separateness"; thinking that we *can* gain something for ourselves alone without regard to others. *At the Feet of the Master* puts it thus:

> Those who are on His side know why they are here and what they should do, and they are trying to do it; all the others do not yet know what they should do, and so they often act foolishly, and try to invent ways for themselves which they think will be pleasant for themselves, not understanding that all are one, and that therefore only what the One wills can ever be really pleasant for anyone.

The root of sin is selfishness. But let us not be too hard on ourselves for that. A certain amount of selfish interest is a necessary protection and instrument of progress for very many people as yet. A child and a savage are often "selfish" through limitation and ignorance. The carapace of *self*-hood protects the growing individuality, as the shell protects the unhatched chick. When the hour is ripe, it is broken and the chicken comes into a wider world. The truly spiritual man has broken the carapace of "I" and "me", but his younger brothers need it to grow and experience. Within the circle of me-and-mine the individuality grows strong and secure until one day the surrounding periphery can be destroyed and yet the centre remains secure.

If a man becomes too "self-centred" he imprisons himself in a very small world, and selfish predatory instincts may make him a danger to others. Hence religions and social groups have framed ethical and moral codes, which sometimes get outworn or are disregarded in revolutionary eras. The Lord Christ Himself laid down no rules which were not in line with natural laws and natural forces. The truth, the fundamental truth, He said, would make men free, and He evoked the free and untrammelled use of the threefold power in man, of mind and heart and action. "Seek," said He, "and ye shall find." With what do we seek, but with the humble, unconditioned, inquiring mind? Intelligence is a God-given power. As before mentioned, it is not the same as the intellect. The storing of "facts", the amassing of "knowledge", the memorizing of great reading, can occur with the use of very little intelligence. Intelligence pierces *through* facts, sees their qualities, relationships, spiritual significance. It is allied to the heavenly *intuition*, "the true Light which lighteth every man that cometh into the world". As Dr. Besant has phrased it, occult study consists less in the amassing of facts than in the creation of *faculty*—faculties of understanding, insight, vision. Pride, acquisitiveness, desire only to know for the sake of knowing and not for the sake of understanding and service of men will prevent this growth of inner faculty. It must be the heart as well as the head that desires wisdom and knowledge. Rightly and wonderfully did King Solomon ask of God to give him "an understanding heart".

So let us seek the True, in everything, in everybody, in every circumstance, with patience, with humility, with love.

Love leads me to that other direction of the Lord Christ: "Ask, and it shall be given you." You cannot "kill" the desire-nature in man. It is the moving force of the universe. At first the soul desires ardently petty, personal, even selfish things; to deny him these is to leave him without hope. But those who are seeking the wisdom of life have wider, purer hopes; they long for comfort, beauty, insight for the race of men, and not for themselves. It is said of a disciple that "not for himself but for the world he lives". In a letter to a disciple a Master of the Wisdom wrote: "You must live for other men and with them, not for or with yourself." So *Light on the Path* tells us to desire ardently, "hunger for such possessions as can be held by . . . the united spirit of life".

But do not let us try that which is as yet beyond our strength. Let us put it another way: learn to love. Think what love is, ever purer and purer forms of it. True love will extirpate pride, egotism, selfishness from our souls. Do not let us want to *be* anything in heaven or earth; only to love and understand.

Lastly comes right action. Thought and desire are not enough. They must find expression in daily life. Let us not be afraid to *show* we love, by little attentions and loving deeds. So often someone we love passes over and we find we have never told him (or her) how we loved him; we have let pass so many little occasions when we could have made him happy with a word or a glance. It is more important to make people happy than to make them " good ". We cannot make them good, for people can only make themselves good, and so to point out their mistakes—except when it is our duty to children and servants—is in most cases not our business.

Says *The Voice of the Silence*: " Self-knowledge [i.e. knowledge of the God within] is of loving deeds the child." And Charles Kingsley wrote in a little girl's album: " Do noble things, not dream them all day long." We can all have our own ideals for living, remembering always that, as we *live* them, those ideals will enlarge and purify, ever leading us onward. But we must never impose them upon other people, nor must we lower them for ourselves because " everybody else does so ". There is a kind of common denominator called public opinion. The best people are always ahead of it, the worst people a long way behind. But always our standards belong to ourselves alone.

Lastly, and mostly, let us be kind. The love-power in so many of us is such a poor, cramped, egotistic copy of the Divine Flame. I think when we come to the last great Gateway, we shall be glad to remember that we have been kind, that we have encouraged, that we have forgiven.

As long as one has not developed a perfect sense of justice one should prefer to err rather on the side of mercy than commit the slightest act of injustice.

MASTER K. H.

Love watcheth, and sleeping, slumbereth not. When weary it is not tired; when straitened it is not constrained; when frightened it is not disturbed; but like a vivid flame and a burning torch, it mounteth upwards, and securely passeth through all.

Whosoever loveth knoweth the cry of this voice.

THOMAS À KEMPIS

CHAPTER XII

WHERE ARE WE AFTER DEATH? THE PROCESS OF DYING

It will not be necessary in these days to spend any time discoursing upon the subject that there *is* a life after death, for most people are already convinced of that truth. There is too much evidence pouring into the world to any longer doubt it. It is true that most of it comes from the Spiritualists. The difference between Spiritualism and Theosophy is this. Theosophy fully recognizes the validity of psychic phenomena, though stating that the cause and meaning of such phenomena is not always rightly understood and evaluated, but Theosophists for the most part do not practise any form of mediumship.

Then how do they know about the other side, it may be asked? By a far more difficult, but also far more accurate and comprehensive way, available only to certain people, possessing an inborn predisposition for such knowledge, who have worked hard in training and developing the power to see and contact the surrounding invisible worlds. Such trained seers note down what they discover with truly scientific patience and accuracy and continually compare notes with each other. In this way the whole vast country upon the other side of death has been explored and mapped out. We will try to epitomize the main findings and conclusions.

The first thing that emerges is the fact that the next life is not away beyond the stars, but here and now, all round us in this same spot of space. Do not say: "I do not believe you because I cannot see it"; but remember that our physical eyes will respond only to a certain limited range of vibrations; they will not register the subtle sights and sounds of a finer, more rapidly vibrating form of matter. For the surrounding invisible worlds are still "material", though the matter of which they are composed is enoromously finer and subtler than physical matter. We may call it the "soul-world", for our souls or psychic selves are already there, interpenetrating and surrounding our physical selves, as the soul or psychic world interpenetrates and surrounds the physical globe, as explained in chapter III.

Death means that the subtler, interpenetrating inner man or soul withdraws from the outer physical sheath, generally from the feet upwards. Death should never be feared, but welcomed, for it is the great liberator, Nature's kindly deliverer from the pains and trials of life. Like sleep, it brings peace and refreshment to the tired soul. Indeed sleep and death have often been compared. "How wonderful is death," writes Shelley "death and his brother sleep!" And Homer describes the passage of the hero to the heavenly places by the twin-bearers, sleep and death. In fact the gateways of sleep, death and deep meditation are the same gateway. In sleep, in death, in deep meditation, the consciousness, the soul, withdraws from its physical counterpart, temporarily in the case of sleep and meditation, permanently in the case of death. Yet there is this difference between sleep and death. Whilst we are away from our bodies through the gateway of sleep, we are still connected with them by a flow of life-magnetism which looks to clairvoyant vision like a thread of silver light. Wherever a sleeper goes upon the other side that thread of light follows him. Through it he immediately awakes if touched. If it be objected that he may be "long way away", let it be remembered, if not understood, that every plane or condition of matter has its own time and space valuations. Picturing these subtle things in physical words we are bound to "materialize" them, to dress them in the well-known phenomena of our familiar physical world.

But when death comes, the silver thread (the birth-cord, if we like, of a new life) is snapped, and so no more return to the body is possible. This may explain the well-known words of *Ecclesiastes*: "Or ever the silver cord be loosed, or the golden bowl be broken." That is another mystery difficult to visualize, and materialized when we do so. Here is its rationale: there is only one Life in all the universe and it is the Divine Life. It throbs and shines in every atom, in every cell, in every form. To a certain very high form of spiritual clairvoyance it looks like an endless, delicate line of light, weaving in lines of light the matrix of every form from the atom to man. This shimmering veil of light and life is like the skeleton which gives form and shape to the living leaf. Within its shining frame-work, the body of a man forms and shapes. It is the cohesive, life-supporting power. When death comes this golden frame-work begins to roll up, cocoon-fashion, from the feet upwards, and the co-ordinating force having thus departed, the atoms and molecules of the body begin to fly apart and go to form part of other forms, animal or vegetable or human. This is the process of disintegration.

But what of the Last Day when we shall rise again in our physical bodies? A moment's thought will convince us that this is an impossibility. It is not the resurrection of the body which is true, but the continual resurrection of the soul in a new and better body. Tennyson says:

> The Lord let the house of a brute to the soul of a man,
> And the man said, "Am I your debtor?"
> And the Lord—"Not yet: but make it as clean as you can,
> And then I will let you a better."

Plato regarded life in the physical body as a grave where men were buried for their sins. Walt Whitman had the same idea. The fact remains that since there is said to be a strict conservation of matter and force in the universe, if reincarnation be not true, and a quite new soul is created every time a child is born, on that mythical Last Day there will not be standing room on the planet nor enough atoms to go round! No, the worn-out vesture of the soul is never resurrected. A new and better body is given to the man when his soul again returns to earth.

Meanwhile the soul, when withdrawn from the physical body, is in the surrounding psychic world, so near and yet unseen. It is not commonly realized that the Greek word *hades*, which is often translated as "hell" in the Bible, does not mean a place of torture at all. It simply means the "unseen", the "invisible". Thus *hades* is all round us, "unseen" only to physical sight.

Let us describe the process of dying, and we will begin with the statement that no one dies before his time unless he takes his own life, or is unduly killed in war. We all have a certain stock of Life-Force like a bank balance, some more than others. When it begins to peter out the end is approaching. Quite often, in the case of very old people, the soul is already turning inwards, and the less controlled and played upon brain-cells repeat automatically old memories and past events. This turning inwards is known upon the other side, and the returning soul is waited for and welcomed. An old lady once said to the writer that she did not wish to die because she did not want to go amongst strangers. "Did you come to strangers when you came back to this life?" I asked her. "Were you unexpected, unwelcomed?"

During life our consciousness is turned outwards, contacting the experiences of life. When the time comes for us to pass on, the consciousness will begin to recede and turn inwards and upwards. So sometimes a dying person will say that the room is receding or that the light is going out. Sometimes as they approach the great gateway the veil between the two worlds will thin, and the dying person becomes conscious of the sights and sounds of the other world. A dying Irish soldier asked a nurse who all the lovely ladies were who surrounded him? They would look lovely to him for they were in the radiant, shining world of the " ever-young ", the Tir-na-og. This same phenomenon happened with my own father, though at that time I did not know what it meant. A day or two before he died he kept telling me that he saw lights, and then he said: " Who are all these people, Clara? You have not introduced me to them."

Whilst I was in Australia, years ago, I used regularly to broadcast on all these subjects, and quite often got letters from listeners as far away as New Zealand. A New Zealand doctor wrote to me to tell me of an old couple on a lonely station, or farm, that he was called out to one night. He found the old man dead when he arrived, but he had his arms outstretched. Inquiring of the wife why this was, she replied: " Oh! sir, we once had a daughter who died when she was seventeen, and just before he went my husband said that he saw her and he held out his arms to her crying: ' Wait for me, Mary, I'm coming '."

Just at passing a very wonderful happening occurs. The consciousness going inwards passes through the subtler portion of the brain where the record of all that happened still exists. It seems to go backwards from the present moment to childhood. Nothing is forgotten. Everything seems to come up again in due order and sequence. A Master of the Wisdom says that the soul identifies itself for a moment with the immortal spiritual divine man, and from that standpoint sees the whole of the life just being quitted, the lessons the soul learnt, where it succeeded, where it failed, and judges accordingly. Hence it is a very solemn moment and should never be disturbed. This will sometimes go on in the consciousness after the body has ceased to breathe. Therefore the Master tells us to step softly, to watch lovingly, besides the bedside of a dying man. A Tibetan scripture tells us to keep still and to whisper lovingly to the dying, for though his ears may not hear, his soul will hear. It is as if, leaving the arena of life, the soul turned and saw in a bird's-eye view the whole of the past life on earth. Sometimes people who have nearly gone over by drowning will tell of a similar experience.

For the first time in life, the etheric part of the physical body separates from its counterpart. It can be seen, and even photographed, hovering over the physical casement for some time. Very soon, however, the soul or psychic self separates again from that. and the consciousness falls into a sleep during which the psychic body is adapted to an independent existence on the other side. The matter of the psychic body arranges itself in concentric sheaths, the coarsest matter on the surface, thus limiting at first the consciousness to that particular stratum of the psychic world. I say "limits the consciousness" because in the soul-world sense-perception is no longer functioning through organs of the five senses, though the psychic counterparts of them are there. The response to stimuli is given by the whole psychic body simultaneously.

But always, on awakening, the soul knows someone is near him, generally someone he knows and loves who has preceded him into that life. He has now passed into the inner life of the soul which to him was "subjective" during life. It is now becoming increasingly "objective". Hence a man builds and conditions by his own subjective powers of thought, desire and imagination the whole of his after-death life. Drawn by the golden thread which binds him to his Inner God, his "Father in Heaven", he is slowly returning heavenwards, "bringing his sheaves with him", that is to say, the summation of the best and most enduring happenings which the spiritual ego is capable of assimilating, and which will unfold into what an Adept called "a concatenation" of happiness-producing events which constitute the soul's rest and compensation for all the darkness and trials of earth. Rightly did the ancient Romans call death "the Gate of Life". As we all pass through that portal, we do not go from life to death, but from life to greater life, ever-increasing, happier life, free from the trials, ills and limitations of earth-life. It is well described by the beloved of the life-prisoner in that wonderful novel of du Maurier's, *Peter Ibbetson.* In it, she comes back after death to her lifelong lover and tells him she awaits him in a world where the worst in us falls gradually below the surface and the best in us comes increasingly to the fore.

Do not fear death. If possible, do not grieve for death. All natural processes are beautiful and God-given, and are accompanied on the inner planes by lovely angelic, or *devic,* forces, the angels of birth and the angles of death. I like the words of the Catholic ritual: "Into Thy Hands I commend my spirit." *Requiescat in pace*, "may he rest in peace". When we know and realize these things, well may we echo St. Paul's triumphant words: "O death, where is thy sting? O gràve, where is thy victory?"

In most persons the process of death is not painful. It is a painless falling into the vast arms of sleep and rest, the "everlasting arms" underneath the worlds. If I am questioned about "death-rattles", etc. I can but reply that this is the reflex action of physical muscles ceasing to function. The consciousness for the most part is unaware of it.

The last thought in death provides the direction the soul takes immediately afterwards. Thus, if a man dies thinking of his family far away, he will appear there almost at once; and if caught sight of is denominated a "wraith". Generally such an appearance seems unconscious because the consciousness is still sleeping.

I remember, during the war, a mother telling me of her little daughter insisting that Daddy was down in the dining-room when the mother knew him to be at the front. Soon afterwards a telegram from the War Office informed her of his death. Another mother told me how one Sunday in church she saw for a moment her son staggering towards her. At that very moment, as a War Office wire told her, he had died in action.

One other war story I must tell, of how young General Congreve sent a message to his mother as he died to ask her to go to his funeral dressed in white, and to have the village church bells ring a wedding-peal. He felt he was to become, as the Chinese say, a "guest of Heaven".

CHAPTER XIII

WHERE ARE WE AFTER DEATH? THE PSYCHIC WORLD

WHAT is life like in the psychic or soul world? Is it anything like life in the physical world? Perhaps this will be better understood if I describe the conditions of matter there. The matter of the psychic world permeates the whole of this physical globe, and because of its extreme tenuity, extends into space enormously beyond it, many thousands of miles if measured by physical standards. Like all forms of matter of any plane it exists in seven degrees of density. As in the human aura the heavier, denser kind of psychic matter tends to drift downwards, below the knees in a human form, as it does towards the centre of the earth in a globe. Thus, on the whole, psychic matter arranges itself in seven concentric spheres interpenetrating and enormously surrounding this world.

Now "psychic" matter is not conditioned by heat or cold, is not resistant or impenetrable as the densest forms of physical matter are. It is instantaneously responsive not to any physical force, but to the subtler impulses of thought, will, emotion and imagination. It is conditioned by these, and all psychic forms, whether houses, scenes, clothes, bodies, are built by these all through. This process has been going on all through the physical life, and is dimly sensed by the interior senses as the "subjective" world of our inner selves. Imagination, meditation, deep thought, will make this inner world more potent and more sensible to the physical man. After death, he *is* that inner man, and that inner world unfolds before him, the subjective becoming more and more objectivized. He is "retreating within", and the process is a long one.

As already stated, immediately after death our inner psychic self arranges itself with the coarsest matter of its constitution outwards. This at first limits the soul's vision to that sub-sphere which corresponds to the soul's outermost covering of psychic matter. Thus every man "goeth to his own place". If a man's life has been predominantly evil, he will awake after death in one of the lower sub-spheres, because the outermost matter of his own psychic body corresponds to it. But only for a time, for gradually the coarser layers wear away, and the better side of a man manifests, bringing him into touch with brighter and more beautiful conditions.

To understand this better, I will describe in general terms the seven sub-spheres of the psychic world. The lowest and densest is below our feet interpenetrating the centre of the earth. It is dark and turgid and dense, the very atmosphere so heavy as to be almost tangible. Nothing living seems to exist there. The scenery is like many a Gustave Dore's picture—vast, bare mountains and plains in a dim and heavy light. No one finds himself there immediately after death, except the exceptionally evil and selfish man, and even for him there is hope. His own diviner self will slowly draw him back, and the days of his purgation and expiation will be ended. One of the best descriptions of this state that I ever came across was in a book, *Gone West*, written many years ago by an Oxford don who was clairvoyant. It describes the experiences after death of a British officer of renown, who was a very wicked man but who had great strength of character. The first glimpse of better things came to him when he saw a gleam of light and followed it. The light was the heart-felt prayers of someone who loved him on earth! It may be noted here that there are always helpers, both among the living and the dead, who descend to the dark places, and render help. It is possible for the higher to descend, but the lower cannot ascend until the hour has come.

The next great sub-plane is co-terminal with the surface of the earth, and some part of it is indeed the psychic counterpart of our life here, reproducing all the objects of this familiar world. It *is* this world, seen from the other side. Every flower and plant, every house, every chair and table, has its psychic counterpart. Suppose, when we were sitting in a physical hall listening to a concert or a lecture, we could close our physical eyes and open our psychic ones. For a moment we would not see much difference.

We are still in the same hall and the same point of space, but are now seeing it from the psychic side instead of the physical side. Soon many differences would strike us, the lambent, living light round every creature and object, the intense and sensible movement of the matter of which they were composed, the flowing, vibrating colour of the atmosphere, the absence of any horizon, or of any body from which light comes as the sun. "And there shall be no night there; and they need no candle, neither light of the sun." (*Rev.*, 22.5). Everything glows with its own light, hence it is a shadowless world. (This is one way in which we may judge whether we are *really* seeing the psychic world, or only a vision projected by our own imagination and wish-fulfilment.)

This is the world where most of us find ourselves when we slip through the gateway of sleep. It is here that during sleep we can contact one newly passed over and bring back the memory imprinted on the brain as a vivid dream.

The other sub-spheres rise higher and further away from earth, and become increasingly more unearthly and difficult to describe. We would be blind and deaf in them, unless our psychic body corresponded. The radiant matter of the psychic world, self-luminous, becomes even more glorious and radiant in these higher worlds. Perhaps these are what the ancient Greeks called the Elysian Fields.

What do we do there, and what is life like there? Now the first thing to remember is that when we are using our psychic bodies, either temporarily or permanently apart from the physical counterpart, we are using a medium which knows neither heat nor cold, hunger or thirst, nor fatigue, pain, deformity or old age. With the loss of a physical body these things are gone. What a relief to be free of an aching, ill, tired body! We are free of it temporarily through the gateway of sleep, and permanently through the gateway of death. The psychic body cannot be ill, tired or old.

But some of us may have seen a " spirit-photograph " of our grandmother who certainly looked old. There are many more factors behind spirit-photography than many spiritualists realize at present, and there is this further fact to be considered. Psychic matter, as before stated, is conditioned by thought. If we have looked in the glass every morning and seen ourselves as " old " we shall carry the thought-habit over with us until gradually we lose it.

Our soul-bodies do not require food and drink. Perhaps some will miss this at first if they have been *too* fond of food! Then their desire will create the simulacrum, but that too will pass. Do we wear clothes, and live in houses? Yes, we wear clothes and we live in houses, but the clothes are not spun on a loom, nor the houses built of bricks and mortar. They are instantly, and in most cases unconsciously, created by a man's thought. The collective thought of many raises many a concert hall, church, laboratory in the other world; matter there, being one veil removed nearer reality, affords fascinating findings and experiences. Having no longer to earn a living, food, clothing and shelter, for himself and his family, a man is free, perhaps for the first time, to turn his attention to what always had interested him, but for which he had no time on earth.

There is no night and day there, no need to go to sleep, except that there are merciful periods of oblivion for newly-arrived and tired souls. Time there is not measured by ticks of the clock, but rather by intensity of experience. Dr. Alexis Carrel, in *Man, the Unknown*, states that even every physical body has its own time-rhythm.

We do not need to use trains and motor cars, for what we think of is immediately present with us. We seem to walk there, but we *can* travel by a mere effort of the will as a bird flies through the air. If this has been discovered by a sleeper, he may remember a vivid dream of "flying". But it cannot be too much emphasized that a man is the *same* man the day after death that he was the day before; the loss of his physical body has not made his character any different.

Of all people on the other side the children have the happiest time. Here is the land of real "make-believe". There we really become Robin Hood or Richard the Lion-Hearted as long as we "hold the thought". Children mature on the other side, unless sometimes, if they die very young, they come back again to earth, quite often as a younger child in the same family. And a "dead" mother meets and plays with her children when they are out of their bodies through sleep. Some little children are psychic, though they often lose the psychic sense as they grow older. A psychic friend of the writer was once travelling in a train with a little girl and her grandmother. The child kept saying that Mummy was there, which annoyed the grandmother. My friend interposed. "The child is speaking the truth," she said, "for I can see her too."

We may ask how we shall recognize each other if the old grow young again and the children mature? Have no fear. "We shall recognize each other under any change," wrote Goethe. The recognition of soul by soul is far deeper, more satisfying and more real than anything we experience on earth, separated so much by the mask of the physical body. All life is more and more happy, free and real as we penetrate and reach each succeeding inner plane of being.

There is the question of heaven and hell; are there such places? There are no *places* anywhere that could thus be designated, but there are soul conditions that could be thus described. Only none of them are eternal; all are temporary in Nature. Man's final home is a heaven beyond his powers of imagination. The spiritual man in him will finally conquer both ignorance and pain. This is the immortal destiny which doth shape our ends, rough-hew them with ignorance and pain meanwhile as we may. To *every* man, even to the worst man in the world—because he has some good in him—comes, after death, a long period of rest and peace and happiness, the compensation to the soul for the darkness and trials of earth.

This is *all* men's divine birthright, and it shall be discussed in the succeeding chapter. To some there is an intervening period of suffering and expiation which takes place upon the psychic plane. That suffering and limitation the man has created for himself during his lifetime. Let us try and visualize how this is done.

First, let us remember that the words " heaven " and " hell " do not mean in reality what we now associate with the words. " Heaven " means illimitable expansion and rest. It is related to the word " haven ". " Hell ", on the other hand, means exactly the opposite. The word, from the Icelandic, means a " hole ", and indicates something shut in, imprisoned. Nowhere in the Christian scriptures, properly translated and understood, is there any teaching of a material hell, or of an *eternal* hell. The Greek word which is translated eternal, everlasting, for ever, really means " for an age ", a span of time certainly coming to an end. Also the Hebrew word *sheol* in the Old Testament is sometimes translated as " hell " and sometimes as " pit " or " grave ". For instance, when Jacob speaks of bringing his grey hairs to the *grave*, and the Psalmist sings: " Thou wilt not leave my soul in *hell*". In the New Testament the word most frequently translated as hell is the Greek word *hades*, which, mentioned before, merely means the " unseen ", the " invisible ". In old England the hole in the wall, near which the mediaeval tailor used to sit cross-legged, and into which he flung his scraps of cloth, was called his " hell ".

Evidently a hell-condition is an imprisoned condition, and the Christ meant *that* when He spoke of one cast into prison who could not come out until he had paid the uttermost farthing. The writer once saw a case like that. I was in America at the time of the execution of the murderess Ruth Snyder. The morning after the execution I saw her quite clearly. She was wringing her hands and moaning: " Why must I die? " As sometimes happens, she had not realized that she was " dead ". All round her, by her own thought-power, she was building all the scenes of the murder, the trial and the execution. Again and again she went through it all. It reminded me of a play acted in New York called " No Exit ". I was so sorry for her that I put my arms round her, but nothing I could do would make her aware of me. She was completely wrapped up in her own thought-pictures. I had to find someone with greater knowledge and power than myself, to break these thought-pictures for her and to teach her not to re-form them. How near to the truth are the ancient Greek myths of Tantalus and Sisyphus.

The " flames of hell " are highly coloured allegorical accounts of the cravings of unholy, unsatisfied desires. It is bad enough when a man cannot satisfy them upon the physical plane. It is many times worse when those fierce desires work through the subtler medium of the psychic body and on that plane they cannot be gratified. One danger is that in the desperate hunt for satisfaction the dead man may find out how to obsess the body of a mediumistic person and thus vicariously obtain satisfaction. If this does not happen, the unfed fires die down after a time and set the man's consciousness free to open out to a much happier vision of the universe. Passion and greed create those hidden fires; intense selfishness makes a prison where a man is shut in upon himself. To all such sorrowing souls let us send the healing forces of our love and prayers.

But as to the vast majority of people, no such fate awaits them after death. Simple, honest, decent, kind people have their after-death life at once beautiful, compensating, full of peace. Do not call them back by undue grief and craving for their beloved presence. They have gone to their happiness and rest, and we shall soon follow them; in the next chapter I will suggest how best to reach and touch their consciousness. Meanwhile there remains one more point to be noted here, the fate of suicides.

Quite rightly is it considered a sin, thus arbitrarily to quit the arena of life. Because the sands of life are not yet run down, the soul is held in the vicinity of the earth until his hour should strike—this is the state the spiritualist would call earth-bound. But much depends upon the *motive* for the act. When a sorely-tried or grief-stricken soul, crazed with pain or fear, takes what seems to him the shortest way out, helpers will surround him and weave protection round him that he may dwell in dreams until his rightful hour shall strike. But if a man does this act merely to escape personal shame or obloquy, his fate is not so happy. To all those we know who have taken their own lives let us send our enduring love and prayers, for those forces avail so much to aid, to cheer, to protect, upon the other side.

CHAPTER XIV

WHERE ARE WE AFTER DEATH? THE HEAVEN WORLD

NOW I come to the most beautiful and entrancing side of our after-death state, where we, most of us, spend by far the greater part of our time between the incarnations. This is our true home where the Eternity in us always resides, and to him we take the best and truest of all our life's experiences. It sounds as if we were two people, but we are *really* him, that growing Divinity, and those other parts of him, so partial, so incomplete, are merely his "shadows", the means by which he gathers the food for his growth. This is the "spiritual" man, the everlasting core of our being. Even the wicked, the very undeveloped man, rebecomes him for a time after death, with the memory of all wickedness and sorrow forgotten, for this Higher Self cannot register that. Returning to the next incarnation, the soul will pick up again the seeds of that past evil, but he will now be stronger to deal with it once more. To the honest and the unselfish and the pure this wonderful time comes very soon indeed after death. Their stay in the psychic realm is short and happy.

But even to the wickedest man there comes a glimpse of heaven some time, because he, too, is an immature god, evolving.

Where is this happy land and is it also " material "? Yes, but of a matter so fine and radiant, so life-giving and happy-making that it cannot be described in physically intelligible terms. This is how a seer with well-trained power of clairvoyance has spoken of it: " A sea of living light, surrounded by every conceivable variety of loveliness in colour and form—the whole changing with every wave of thought that he sends out from his mind, and being indeed, as he presently discovers, only the expression of his thought in the matter of the plane. . . . For that matter is of the very same order as that of which the mind-body is composed, and therefore when that vibration of the particles of the mind-body which we call a thought occurs, it immediately extends itself to this surrounding mental matter . . . There is nothing conceivable of loveliness in earth or sky or sea which is not there with a fullness and intensity beyond all power of imagination; but out of all this splendour of living reality each man sees only that which he has within himself the power to see." That is, each man sees that which he has evolved the ability to respond to.

The ancient Greeks called it the Isles of the Blest, where everything that a soul had dreamt of, idealized and longed for, comes true. Here, they say: " The air is serene and soft, full of celestial light, clothing all things in transfigured beauty. Here are majestic groves, verdant meadows, blooming gardens. Here are to be found those heroes who had died for their country, priests who had led a pure life, artists who had embodied pure beauty, poets who had never degraded their muse. Here, each renewed the joys he formerly delighted in, the husband rejoined his wife, friendships were renewed, even the charioteer found his beloved horses again."

The afore-quoted modern seer also says that it is a land of absolute bliss, with an indescribable vitality, confidence and increased power. There is nothing like it here but the life of a happy childhood increased a thousandfold. No evil can find entrance there, or sorrow.

Let us put it in the words of the Christian scriptures: "And God shall wipe away all tears from their eyes; and there shall be no more death, neither sorrow, nor crying, neither shall there be any more pain."

Or, as St. Paul expresses it: "Eye hath not seen, nor ear heard, neither have entered into the heart of man, the things which God hath prepared for them that love him." It means those who love the Beautiful, the True and the Good in life.

Where is this heaven? Here, all around us, unseen by mortal eyes, but glimpsed in the ecstasies and dreams of Saints. The trials, the efforts, of earth, are but the seeds which produce such lovely flowers in the air of heaven.

Says the Lord Buddha: "Many thousand myriads of systems of worlds beyond this is a region of bliss called Sukhāvati. This is the Devachan (i.e. land of the Gods).

Its divine udambara flower casts a root in the shadow of every earth, and blossoms for all those who reach it. Those born into this blessed region are truly felicitous; there is no more grief or sorrow, in that cycle, for them."

This, again, is the land the Christ spoke of when He told us that the Kingdom of Heaven lay deep within us. Says *Light on the Path*: " Listen to the song of life . . . At first you may say: ' It is not there; when I search I find only discord.' Look deeper . . . At the very base of your nature you will find faith, hope and love."

How wonderfully does Wordsworth describe it in *Laodamia*:

He spake of love, such love as spirits feel
In worlds whose course is equable and pure;
No fears to beat away—no stripes to heal—
The past unsighed for and the future sure;
Spake as a witness, of a second birth
For all that is most perfect upon earth.
Of all that is most beauteous, imaged there
In happier beauty; more pellucid streams,
An ampler æther, a diviner air,
And fields invested with purpureal gleams.
Climes which the sun, which sheds the brightest day
Earth knows, is all unworthy to survey.

All this wonderful world is founded upon the true love-nature in man. St. John the Divine said: " Beloved, let us love one another: for love is of God; and every one that loveth is born of God, and knoweth God. He that loveth not knoweth not God; for God is love." Shall we put it the other way round and say: Love, pure selfless love, is God. As the real heart of us is Divinity, that Love is there, growing from life to life and creating for us between the incarnations a glowing, glorious heaven-life. The flowers of love that bloom so gloriously in our heaven-lives are born of seeds sown now on earth, and there are four main varieties, or, if another simile is preferred, there are four main gateways into heaven. What are these four seeds? Some people sow one, and others all of them.

The first seed that every one sows is the seed of unselfish human love of friends and relations. This means that every soul after death lives through what a Master of the Wisdom called a long concatenation of glorious event in which every one they have ever loved is vividly present with them. But it may be asked, how can that be? If my mother, who died many years ago, is now in the heaven world, how can she have me who am here on earth? She no longer has your physical presence, but your spiritual self. She is nearer to you than ever before, because she does not have to get at you through the mask of the physical body. Spirit is responding to Spirit, and down here we cannot imagine how infinitely more wonderful and satisfying such converse is. This is the plane of the "communion of Spirit", where no misunderstanding or misapprehensions are possible. Instead of trying to get a message through a medium, keep still some Sunday afternoon and try to "feel" the warmth of union which reflects into our hearts from the heavenly places. It is well to be loved and remembered by someone there.

The second seed we will call the seed of religious idealism. Some people have that by nature and some have not. Such temperaments worship the Platonic Good, nearly always through some human form which renders God near and dear to them. Thus an ardent Christian will worship the Lord Christ; a fervent Buddhist that great Brother of men, the Lord Buddha. What have they done during life? By countless acts of devotion and adoration, by myriad thoughts flying to the object of their devotion, they have built a wondrous thought-form in their interior world, and the Great Original of that thought knows it and fills His picture with Himself, so that it seems to the devotee after death that his Lord is with him, wearing the familiar appearance under which he had always pictured Him. He is indeed " absent from the body, and present with the Lord ". That is heaven indeed for the truly religious man!

Now, some people naturally look upwards to the One, whilst others more often look downward over the many. This is the temperament of the philanthropist, pre-eminently the lover of humanity. Sometimes a great reformer is of this ilk. Not for the sake of fame or gain, but for the happiness of men he works. He naturally comes into touch after death with the greatest lovers of mankind who exist, the Perfected Men, the Elder Brothers of the Race, and from that contact learns wider and truer views and comes back to the next earth-life with truer vision and wider opportunities to help. This is the third seed which men sow.

The fourth I will call the seed of the love of truth and beauty. Here are the souls who worship the true —scientists, philosophers, discoverers of truth. In a world two veils removed and nearer to Reality, their vision of the eternal laws of the universe is free and untrammelled. When they return to the next incarnation they will bring a far-away memory of that vision, and that will cause them to seek for it again here, if haply they may find it. But never here will that vision entirely reveal itself, only glimpses here and there.

But the soul that loves beauty, and finds in God the Beautiful, the apotheosis of his deepest desires? This is to be the artist of varying degrees—whether as expressed through words and idea in true poetry, through sound in music, colour in pictures, form in sculpture and architecture. There is a special Order of Creation that comes into play here, an Order of Evolution that never touches the dense earth and so has no physical body. Radiant, untouched by sin and sorrow, this is the heavenly order of the Angelic Kingdom, or as the East would name them, the Devas or the " Shining Ones ". John Bunyan used the same term. They are not human, nor do they follow the same method of evolution as we do. They are the embodiments and directors of all the natural forces in the universe, and are the natural priests of the Beautiful. All beauty, whether of colour, sound, form or idea, is an invocation to them. All artists of any degree, owe the main part of their inspiration to them. This is easily to be felt, if not seen. Think of a church in which the organ is pealing, or a great concert hall in which a symphony orchestra is playing. To the right temperament the music brings solace, refreshment, inspiration. On the wings of sound his soul rises above the pre-occupations of earth. His tired nerves are soothed, his soul filled with indescribable bliss. This is because, as Browning wrote, music is a language which " we musicians know ". And when we speak this language the Devas of Sound draw near, bringing with them their atmosphere of peace and upliftment.

One of the Theosophical investigators found a young boy in the heaven world, who had been on earth a chorister in some Minster. He often had to sing a solo anthem in the church, and opposite his stall in the choir was a little stained-glass window with a picture of St. Cecilia, the patron saint of music, playing an organ. This figure grew very real to the boy, and Sunday after Sunday he sang to his beloved St. Cecilia. After death at an early age he found himself in a lovely world with his beloved St. Cecilia, looking just as she had looked in the window. The little boy's thought and imagination had created the form, but it was ensouled by what the East calls a Gandharva, a mighty Angel of Sound. In the next earth-life the boy's musical power will be greatly increased.

This is how we grow in beauty of character, in capacity and power, life after life, with longer and longer heaven-lives in between. By far the greater part of our existence is spent in these happy worlds. Life on earth is but a needed probation. Three score years and ten here, and hundreds of years there. Again Browning writes, with the intuition of a poet: " On the earth the broken arcs; in the heaven, a perfect round."

It may be argued that if life is so lovely there we would never want to return. Every one returns because his immortal spiritual life *wants* to. *Tanha*, the thirst for sentient existence, will arise in him again and lead him back to another incarnation, but this will be when all the forces generated in the last earth-life have found their complete fulfilment in heaven, and the causes of that fulfilment are exhausted.

Meanwhile, when those we love quit us through the gateway of death, do not let us speak of them as lying in the grave. Nothing is in the grave except the worn-out vesture of the man. We may treasure it because he wore it, as mothers treasure little shoes their children once wore, but it is no longer of any use to him. He is free of the ills of life, and living a so much wider, freer, happier life than whilst on earth. Would we call him back? Ah! no. We shall follow him and he will be there to greet us when our turn comes. Always we may send to him our undying love and thought, for in that subtler world such forces cannot fail to reach and bless.

Well may we echo the lovely words of the poet Shelley in *Adonais*:

> Peace! peace! he is not dead, he doth not sleep:
> He hath awakened from the dream of life.

CHAPTER XV

SLEEP AND DREAMS

It has been stated before that the gateways of death, sleep and deep meditation are virtually the same gateway. When our body falls asleep, it is because the real consciousness, the soul or psychic counterpart, has left it for a time. Since that psychic counterpart permeates and surrounds the physical body, it is easy to picture its withdrawal, either sideways or from the feet upwards. Similar psychic matter from the surrounding plane rushes in at once to fill the temporary void, but the real man has gone.

Now it will be objected that no one ever saw themselves fall asleep, in other words, were conscious of the withdrawal. It is not common, but the writer has met several people who temporarily or permanently had that power. In most cases an isolated instance occurs once or twice during life, as in the case of the young Australian girl who described how one night she found herself outside her body, looking down on it lying in the bed. At the other side of the room she saw her mother's form also sleeping. "Then," in her own words, "I leant over my body and sort of melted into it (osmosis) and I awoke."

Then there is the instance of a hard-headed Yorkshire businessman who all his life long had left and entered his body consciously. This man, evidently a little psychic, also told the writer of a curious experience he had once whilst waiting in a train at Chester. Suddenly, through the modern scene, like a dissolving view in a cinema, came a living moving scene of the Roman colonization of Britain. Roman and ancient British workmen were moving everywhere, and the narrator was particularly impressed by the handsome looks of the Roman overseer.

Whether we can remember it or not, we *do* all leave our bodies at night, and the consciousness of the psychic plane, incompletely and often symbolically brought through into the physical brain, constitutes most though not all " dreams ".

Let us first consider what we can really do at night and then consider the problem of how this may be registered by the physical brain, which, of course, we do not take away with us. Free of the body, and in the spatial conditions of the other side, we may visit places on this earth, seeing them, of course, from the standpoint of their psychical counterparts. For it must be remembered that the psychic plane on which most people find themselves during sleep is the one which reproduces this world, and is in fact this world seen from the other side.

As soon as we leave our bodies we find ourselves still in the same house. Perhaps we " float " down the stairs and out into the streets. I say " float " because the tenuous psychic body does not necessarily need to walk, but propelled by the will can travel at a great speed through the psychic atmosphere. Some people have found this out, though large numbers still retain the physical habits of thought which condition them on the other side. Such people as have discovered it may relate in the morning that they had dreamt they were " flying ". This is a well-known and common phenomenon, explained away by a French scientist as becoming conscious, at the moment of waking, of the rhythmic expansion and contraction of the lungs!

Some people have " vivid dreams " of places and conditions they have never seen here, and some find themselves visiting a spot on earth that they had known before in dreams. I remember a young officer in the first part of the World War telling me that, ordered to take over a certain segment of the line, he found he knew perfectly every section of it! He had prospected during sleep. " For sleep has sights as clear and true," wrote Shelley, " as any waking eyes can view."

At the same time we meet people, those who, as ourselves, are temporarily on the psychic plane, or those who have recently come there through the gateway of death. For instance, suppose before going to bed we were engaged with a number of people in a most interesting conversation. We are likely to continue it on the other side. Those who are on the psychic plane through the gateway of death are likely to move to more glorious and subtle realms soon, which explains the fact that dreams of them cease after a while.

There are one or two differences between one who is only asleep and one who has died, as mentioned before. Wherever a sleeper goes the shining line of life-magnetism follows him. Spatial terms are different there, so if the sleeper is awakened he is instantaneously back. Sometimes something very impressive or alarming on the other side will send a sleeper back with a shock.

With one veil of heavy matter removed, we may find during sleep the solution of a problem which eluded us by day; hence the well-known story of the mathematician who woke with the solution of a difficult mathematical problem in his mind. The composer Mozart is also reported to have said that he brought through a certain composition as a chord which gradually unfolded into a symphony or sonata. This fact has given rise to common sayings such as the advice to "go to bed and sleep on it", and the aphorism "the night brings counsel".

We may also occasionally be warned in what is known as a "prophetic dream". Before any event crystallizes on this plane, the gathering inner forces behind it can be seen looming on the psychic plane. This may be caught sight of by a sleeper, and duly impressed on the waking brain. When such a dream occurs it must not be concluded that it is *bound* to occur on the physical plane exactly as in the dream. For at any moment the man can introduce new factors which will make it work out in another way.

I have said that the majority find themselves on the counterpart of the physical plane during sleep. But the trained and evolved soul is free to go much further. He may visit lower planes as a helper, or visit higher ones for learning and inspiration. There is on the other side a band of trained helpers, both among the sleepers and the dead, who are taught how best to help the "spirits in prison", how to bring comfort and explanation to the ignorant newly dead, how to comfort and help unseen, sorrowing relatives; and the highly trained of them may also bring visible aid on the physical plane. Those who desire to join that band of invisible helpers, and have characteristics which can be used, will be drawn in and trained; but it demands great love of men and great self-control, for all emotions and thoughts on the other side are so much more vivid and potent. The whole band is under the direction of an Adept, and is divided into companies each in charge of an experienced worker, probably a disciple of an Adept. This band not only helps the newly dead, the earth-bound souls, the distressed on earth, but puts high and inspired thoughts into the minds of pure-minded statesmen, writers, servers of humanity of all kinds.

The strongest of this band can descend into the lower planes which are truly the abode of souls in prison, bringing help, illumination and hope. They can also ascend to higher planes, where true occult instruction is given. Only the faint shadow of this is ever given on earth, and one proof that a man is receiving this instruction at night will be seen in his gradually widening consciousness and mind, and in his deepening and ever-growing charity of heart.

Quite a number of people have found their way to these planes of enlightenment at night, and the memory in the physical brain sometimes shows itself as the memory of vast halls, wearing the appearance of Greek temples with pillars and shallow steps and glowing, changing spaces within, where living pictures and shining " words " flash before the sleeper. *Light on the Path* calls it the Hall of Learning. It was there that the writer, Mabel Collins, saw the ancient aphorisms which are transcribed in that book.

When we fall asleep, as when we die, we go where our heart lies, as is well described in Alice Meynell's poem: "I run, I run, I am gathered to thy heart." Sometimes intense love and desire can bring about results that would ordinarily require trained and expert occult knowledge. A young officer in the war told me how one night he was having supper with three other men in a ruined cottage on a sector of the front, when he suddenly heard his mother's voice—she being at the time asleep in England—say urgently: " Come out! Come out at once! " Twice she spoke with increasing urgency. So impressed was he that he stepped outside, and immediately a shot fell on the cottage and killed the other three men. His mother must have seen that " looming " on the other side, having gone to her son as soon as she left the body, and in her intense anxiety to save him managed to make her voice audible.

The writer is convinced that the phenomenon of the " Comrade in White ", reported from all fronts during the first World War, was due to the materialization of an Adept, thus bringing in wounded soldiers who would not otherwise probably be found.

Now, how do we "remember" these wonderful happenings outside the body. Out of the body we remember all the days *and* nights. In the body, only the days. That is because we do not take our brain away with us, and to be able to impress the subtle sights and sounds of an inner world upon it when we awake, requires a sensitive brain, well controlled and left at peace. Whilst we are away from it, thought-currents and desire-surgings from the outer world surge through it, or at least such outer thought-currents as it would normally respond to. Any acute physical disturbance, such as a tooth-ache or indigestion, will cause automatic activity in the brain, causing it to repeat disjointed vibrations experienced during the day. These account for the foolish, disjointed dreams which seem to mean nothing. They also prevent the full memory of the night's experiences coming through. It is as if the soul coming back and trying to write on the brain what has happened finds it is already scribbled over. A true word here and there may be distinguished. Keeping peaceful, going to sleep on a high thought, and the determined will to "remember" are potent helps. True memories are so subtle, so quickly evanescent that they disappear almost at the moment of waking, and to recover them here is like trying to hear the strains of a violin in the midst of a big brass band. Yet it can be done.

Another type of pure brain dream is brought about by some physical impact. The subtler portion of the brain has an extraordinary power of dramatization and is also quite oblivious of the time factor. A well-known instance is that of the famous writer who dreamt that he was imprisoned during the French Revolution for three weeks and finally executed by the guillotine, waking up at that very moment to find that the curtain pole had fallen across his neck! In that one moment his brain had dramatized the whole long story!

There is one hall-mark of a scrap of true memory, and that is its extraordinary vividness, for on the other side, as before stated, we think more swiftly and feel much more vividly. But because so much on the other side has no distinct parallels here, memories often come through in more or less symbolic form. This gives rise to the old custom of consulting dream books. Only most people have their own system of symbology which does not always square with the dream books. Probably this department of our dream-life is where the psycho-analyst delves, for the higher aspect of ourselves can and does indicate, to his more material representative, factors which cause trouble and should be removed. Sometimes this has a purely physical foundation, for example, to dream your teeth fall out generally indicates digestive trouble.

There are certain common symbols employed by all dreamers, the common ones of losing a train, appearing unclothed in public places, plunging into stormy or dark water, or, on the contrary, sailing over a calm, blue expanse, and seeing flocks of white birds flying overhead. The first three examples are anxiety dreams indicating hidden fears and suspenses. Stormy or dark water indicates the disturbed condition of the dreamer's own psychic state, the agitated undulations of his own aura. The calm, blue waters mean the opposite, and flying white birds always indicate hopes and possibilities, as also does, sometimes, the common dream of holding a new-born baby in our arms.

Dreams are certainly indicative of psychological conditions. I once knew a prosperous baker and his wife, whose only son had emigrated to the United States. Nothing would content the mother but to get her husband to follow him. But she took with her her narrow and exclusively British outlook. Consequently she did not get on well with her new American surroundings and acquaintances. I met her in America, and she told me of her nightly dreams where she was always in darkened rooms with the shutters up and falling over dusty, cumbersome furniture. I suggested to her that this indicated her own frame of mind, which refused to regard alien ways and customs sympathetically and clung tenaciously to mental luggage which did not belong to her new life. She took what I said to heart, and some time later, when I passed that way again, told me that now her dreams were much better. The shutters were open, and much of dusty furniture gone.

How can we know whether we ever reach the higher, more spiritual realms of life, when free of our body at night? Generally, not by pictorial memory, for we have been too far away for that, but by a deep sense of bliss and peace on awakening.

Remember that the last thought, both before sleep and death, is of paramount importance; it constitutes the immediate pathway of the soul when quitting the body. Therefore let us leave outside our bedroom doors, if we can, our worries, troubles and all ugly thoughts. Do we desire to visit a beloved one who is here or who has passed on? Ah! we can. Once at a concert in the Queen's Hall in London I sat listening to a concert. A singer sang such beautiful words to us that I copied them down from the programme. Here they are:

When I am dreaming and the wide world sleeps,
Then shall my soul from out this prison flee,
Strong and immortal o'er dividing deeps,
When you shall call for me.

Love's sweet communion we will hold apart,
E'en though between us mighty oceans roll;
Though tongues be silent heart shall speak to heart,
And soul respond to soul.

And here I cannot forbear from quoting those charming little verses by the poet Coleridge:

If I had but two little wings
And were a little feathery bird,
To you I'd fly, my dear!
But thoughts like these are idle things,
And I stay here.

But in my sleep to you I fly
I'm always with you in my sleep;
The world is all one's own.

But then one wakes, and where am I?
All, all alone.

Sleep stays not, though a monarch bids;
But I love to wake at break of day,
And though my sleep be gone,
Yet, while 'tis dark, one shuts one's lids
And still dreams on.

CHAPTER XVI

THE RETURN TO INCARNATION

How do we come back to life, and are we conscious of the process? It is a very beautiful occasion. Let me try to describe it as clearly as I can.

The first thing to remember is that we have lost both our physical and psychical vestures, and are now pure spirit. The spiritual self has a glorious, radiant "body", too subtle, too tenuous, too other-worldly to be properly imaged by a physical brain. It is this immortal man, who grows from life to to life by the sublimated experiences taken back to him by his evanescent personalities, that enjoys the bliss of the long heaven-life within the veil, so to say, of his last personality. The "concatenation of events" which composed that heaven-life comes to an end at last, because the seeds sown in earth-life which produced it flowered and passed. Then awakes in that spiritual Self the thirst for sentient existence, that he may gain still more material for growth. It is this spiritual hunger which leads a man back to incarnation. His glance turns earthwards.

Although he has lost his last physical body by death, and his last psychic self by gradual sloughing off, so to say, he yet retains one atom of each condition of matter which constitutes the nucleus by which he can return. These " permanent atoms " store the capacity to vibrate in response to any vibration that they have ever experienced. Sometimes from those sub-conscious storages sudden upsurges come. For instance, the night-fears of some children are really upsurging memories of millions of years ago when primitive man hid in fear from his pre-historic animal co-dwellers. There are three permanent atoms which a man carries with him always, belonging to the physical, emotional and mental planes of being. During life they are generally centred in either the head or the heart, a tiny, shining, scintillating triad. If it be asked how a *physical* atom can appear in the spiritual worlds, let it be remembered that the conditions of matter *interpenetrate* each other, and that progress after death is not away and beyond, but within and within.

As soon as the spiritual man turns his glance earthwards, his mental and emotional atoms (or whatever we can call them) awake and begin to vibrate and thrill. This in itself is a magnetic attraction, so there collects round the scintillating little bodies a new and nascent mental and emotional self similar in make-up and material to the mental and emotional selves with which the man was equipped at the close of his last incarnation. The matter is not formed and organized yet. The coming life will do that. It is comparable to the assembling of bricks, mortar and wooden frames when a house is to be built. Life will build the house.

Now, when we come to the *physical* atom, something different happens, because the physical body and the physical life are pre-eminently the domain of *karma*. This is where the Lords of Karma, the *Lipika*, come into action. The Lords of Karma are not human. They are mighty Devic Intelligences, so tremendous and so great that the imagination can hardly conceive of Them. And They do not regard us as "persons", Mary Jones and Thomas Smith, etc.; They are only aware of the forces which we produce on the outer and inner planes by our thoughts, desires and actions. To Them it is like a vast sum which They must solve. The disharmony which They must solve is caused by man's *personal* thought, desire and action, and when a man faces his karma bravely, and learns unselfishness and impersonality (*the root of which is love*), They look on him as Their co-operator, and reward him by sending *more* personal problems, coming from his past, to deal with and solve.

These Lipika, or Recorders, as They are called in the East, guard the great Book of Life, called there the Ākāshic Records. We have the same idea in the Christian scriptures in the Recording Angel and the Book of Life from which men are judged. We write in that Book ourselves every minute of the day, and this is how we do it. For a moment let us come back to the thought of the universe being a wonderful harmony of vibrating wave-lengths. Professor Oliver Reiser, Professor of Philosophy in Pittsburgh University in America says: "The most awesome discovery of the human mind is the discovery of the reliability and underlying harmony of the processes of the natural universe." Every action, every word, produces an undulatory movement. These set up synchronous vibrations in the subtle matter of the interpenetrating psychic world, physical sound there showing as colour. (I once knew a violinist who always saw flashes of colour as he played his violin.) This again sets up finer correlations in still subtler worlds. This is also true of our desires, emotions and thoughts. Thus the thoughts, desires and actions of man resound from plane to plane finally reaching that finest film of matter called by the Eastern sages the Ākāsha. Here it all imprints itself and is for ever happening, for this is the world of Eternal, Timeless Now. This is the Centre of Life, our sequence of events being upon the periphery of the Wheel of Life.

From that self-written record, the Lords of Karma choose that amount of harmony or disharmony caused by a man in the past which he may be presumed able to deal with in the coming life. There are three main kinds of this personal reaction to be dealt with. There is, first, the running karma of everyday events, results coming from causes generated yesterday or some time ago. We should not, for instance, attribute to the karma of a past life such things as minor ailments resulting from wrong living, or antagonism and failures resulting from our own selfishness or incapacity or sloth in this present life. Such everyday karma is generated in this life. The second kind of karma is that which comes from the past and shows as inborn tendencies and weaknesses, and as the major, unexpected events which suddenly occur. These, I expect, could be more or less delineated in a horoscope. It includes the nation, the family a man is born into, the character, opportunities and capacities he brings with him, and the coming life's leading events. In the words of the Prophet Mohammed, "The fate of every man is hung round his neck at birth"; part of that fate is his new physical body, with its environment.

The Lords of Karma here make a kind of plan, which is delivered from higher to lower intelligences until it finally materializes in the form of a little building intelligence upon the subtle side of the physical plane. This intelligence builds the new body of the incoming soul within the mother, taking the materials, according to the plan, from both the father and the mother.

It is well to note that all natural processes are brought about by unseen, invisible intelligences. There are the angels of birth, as well as the angels of death. These angelic or devic forces put the returning Ego or soul in touch with his new body at that time before birth which is called "quickening". H. P. Blavatsky writes: "The Ego wedges itself into the brain and senses of the foetus at the completion of its seventh month, but the Higher Manas (Mind of the Ego) does not unite itself with the child before the completion of the first seven years of its life" (*The Secret Doctrine* III.511). She also writes (*S. D.*, II.198): "One by one the foetus assumes the characteristics of the human being, the first flutter of the immortal breath passes through its being:

it moves; . . . and the divine essence settles in the infant frame, which it will inhabit until the moment of physical death, when man becomes a spirit."

After birth the little building intelligence still continues to attend the child, forming a kind of Guardian Angel until a moment arrives, generally during the sixth or seventh year, when the child's own Higher Manas, or true mind of the soul, descends, so to say, and takes charge, the immortal Ego now becoming the true Guardian Angel of the new personality.

But "not in entire forgetfulness" do we come. As the personality, when quitting the arena of earth-life, sees the whole past life with its dominant impulses and meaning, so, on return, does the immortal Ego glimpse the form and meaning of the coming earth-experience, sometimes more than one such. This shows in the new brain as "innate" ideas and convictions. Sir Francis Bacon wrote that he had always conceived of himself as born to be of service to mankind, and in Maurice Maeterlinck's famous fantasy, *The Blue Bird*, the children come to the mothers with a knowledge of their future destiny.

The third form of karma, sometimes called the "piled-up" karma, is outstanding debts from the past, kept away from a man for many lives until he is spiritually mature enough to learn from them.

CHAPTER XVII

EDUCATION IN THE LIGHT OF OCCULTISM

I THINK the first thing we should all try to realize is that our child *is not ours*. Travelling over the world for more than fifty years, again and again have I seen the awful evil of possessive motherhood and, sometimes but not so often, possessive fatherhood. These deluded people, satisfying their own need for emotional satisfaction and expansion at the expense of their child's soul, are fully persuaded that they " love " their children. In reality they love only themselves, but it takes a big character to be able to see that in oneself, and most people are not " big ". A child does not belong to us. We did not create him, form his character, give him his capacities. These things he created for himself by lives of experience in the past. He comes to us because that past merits such and such surroundings and opportunities and because personal links with him from that past are calling him.

It may be said that the Lords of Karma have a threefold problem with each returning soul:

1. The next step on the evolutionary ladder which would naturally follow;

2. That may be hindered or complicated by the personal merits and demerits of the past;

3. The strong personal link with other souls of love, and alas! sometimes of hate. Out of these three the right child comes to us.

It must also be remembered that the new mental and emotional sheaths of the child are not yet co-ordinated and organized, though the *seeds* of past mental and emotional capacities are there. Thus, the " aura " of a tiny child is almost colourless. Life's experiences will unfold and develop these hidden capacities, and during early years the example and unseen influences of his parents and surroundings are of such amazing force that there is quite a great deal of truth in the saying: " Give me a child until he is seven years old and all the world may do what they will with him afterwards."

The atmosphere and environment of a little child requires three things, security, peace and love. Dissensions, uncertainties, injustices work untold harm to a child's soul. When I was a little child myself I used to wonder why grown-ups treated one with so little respect. A child should always be treated with kindness, consideration and *respect*. How many times are children told not to be " naughty " without in the least understanding what the word implies, until perhaps they discover that it mostly means not being a nuisance to grown-up people!

Before birth a child is mostly influenced through its mother. Therefore a happy, peaceful, expectant mother, surrounded by beauty and simplicity, tends to produce a beautiful child. Again a child should be wanted, and loved, before it comes. People have often noted the high percentage of beauty and health among "love" children. Mary Roberts Rinehart, in her autobiography, *My Story*, writes that when working in a hospital as a nurse:

> There came the conviction which I have never changed; that the real sins are those of the spirit and not those of the body. One thing was strange. The "love" children were beautiful. Where the parents had loved, the child was lovely, whether born in marriage or without. Even today, when I see a beautiful child, I think of that. It enters into no system of eugenics that I know about, but it is true nevertheless. The best child is the product of some strange, unrecognized harmony between the parents.

After birth the child is laid open to the influences of the world, but this should be not quite completely at first, only in successive degree. I am personally against the modern habit in hospitals of keeping babies away from their mothers, except at feeding times. Primitive mothers know this, as do all animals. I remember visiting a miner's wife who had just had a baby. To show me the child, she dived down under the bed-clothes and fished him up from the bottom of the bed. I wondered how he could breathe there, yet perhaps she was right. Madame Montessori has the same thoughts. She says a new-born baby should be kept close to its mother. Otherwise it suffers from the "shock of birth".

For the first seven years of a child's life he is exposed to mostly *physical* impacts. His business is to learn to contact the physical plane. The mental and emotional capacities are in the background. Therefore quite naturally colour and form attract him and he wants to touch and handle everything. Do not expect much mental or emotional response from a very little child. The best thing the parents can do for him is to give him good physical habits and provide him with security and peace. To excite too much mental or emotional response is harmful to a young child. How often do little wonders grow into very ordinary people. Do not expect reasoning powers as yet. Do not ask a child if he " loves Mummy ". It only bewilders him.

Towards the seventh year a great change will often become apparent, generally coincident with the coming of the second teeth. It may not be always so desirable a change in a mother's eyes. Her little angel may suddenly begin to develop a will of his own, and characteristics hardly observed before. This means the descent of the child's own Ego, and the departure of the little guardian spirit. The child is now approaching the age of responsibility. Perhaps for this reason the Greek Church holds that no child under the age of seven can commit mortal sin.

During the next seven years the child's emotional nature pre-eminently unfolds, reaching around fourteen years, the age of puberty, when the sex-nature begins to mature. This period demands emotional contacts, playmates, friendships, hero-worship. Happy is the child who has a noble grown-up he can *truly* love and trust. This is the age for images and parables, tales, religion and art.

From fourteen onwards the mental nature comes more into action, and the sex-nature goes on maturing. But in the development of the mental nature, do not let the emphasis lie upon criticism, competition, rivalry, but rather upon generous appreciation and admiration of others. This is where so often a father's or a mother's personal ambition works havoc. Our son's or daughter's *own* need, their generous sharing in and appreciation of another's success and achievement, are far more necessary than that a parent's pride in them be satisfied.

With the maturing sex-nature, secrecy, shame and misinformation work lasting harm. Sex-aberrations rarely occur in those who have known true love and freedom in their early years. Doctors and psychologists have discovered that most sex-problems and perversions arise from starved and frustrated hearts. Starved hearts also mean lack of imagination in older years. Max O'Rell said that many a young man, passing through his hands at the University, failed of what they might have achieved because they were emotionally starved.

It takes so many years before the incoming Ego becomes completely immersed in matter, quite often not till a man approaches thirty years of age. How extraordinarily true are the intuitions of a great poet. All that I have been trying to say is summed up in the wonderful words of Wordsworth's *Ode on . . . Intimations of Immortality*:

> Our birth is but a sleep and a forgetting:
> The Soul that rises with us, our life's Star,
> Hath had elsewhere its setting,
> And cometh from afar:
> Not in entire forgetfulness,
> And not in utter nakedness,
> But trailing clouds of glory do we come
> From God, who is our home:
> Heaven lies about us in our infancy!
>
> Shades of the prison-house begin to close
> Upon the growing boy,
> But he beholds the light, and whence it flows,
> He sees it in his joy;
> The youth, who daily farther from the east
> Must travel, still is Nature's priest,
> And by the vision splendid
> Is on his way attended;
> At length the man perceives it die away,
> And fade into the light of common day.

But there are some people in whom it never quite dies away, and they are the young in heart, whose idealism survives the assaults of life.

But one thing more must I plead; let us permit our children to be *free*, free to be themselves, to grow in their own way, to gather their own experience, to have their own native idealisms. They cannot begin too soon to take part in human life. Chinese children are always with their parents, taking part in whatever their elders do, and never in the way; and so the children grow in happiness and usefulness. Let them learn early how to do everything themselves, watch father at work, lending him a helping hand, help mother in the house (*little* children like this better than when they are older), watch builders, plumbers and carpenters at work—all this is food for the inquiring mind and active hands. Let them find out everything. Do not destroy the joy of discovery in them by saying: "Let mother do it." Then the children will never be bored (Do we realize the depths of boredom children suffer from?) and will not develop anti-social compensations of a frustrated Ego.

The children I am sorry for are the children out of contact with real life, and surrounded by masses of expensive toys which do not compensate for the lack of exercise of their creative capacity. Sometimes these children become very sad psychological cases. Has not such a child often said to us: "Tell me what I can *do*!" I once made a poor little rich boy happy by telling him to go and help the footman polish the windows.

Let them be in touch with life as much as possible, learn to ride, swim, drive a car, and above all understand and care for animals as friends and not as mere pets. A dog is the natural companion of a boy.

So many parents demand the confidence of their children. To gain it they even make the mistake of trying to be their children's playmates and equals. There is a natural difference between youth and maturity. Where love and trust reigns, not on demand, but spontaneously, confidence exists. We must *win* our children's love and respects by being worthy of it, not make the common mistake of supposing it is our natural heritage.

Love and courage—what else matters in life if we can help our children to these! I will close this chapter with the wise words of H. P. Blavatsky:

> Children should, above all, be taught self-reliance, love for all men, altruism, mutual charity, and more than anything else, to think and reason for themselves. We should reduce the purely mechanical work of the memory to an absolute minimum, and devote the time to the development and training of the inner senses, faculties and latent capacities. . . . We should aim at creating *free* men and women, free intellectually, free morally, unprejudiced in all respects, and above all things, *unselfish*.

A too great burden of memory in early stages stunts the growing, delicate, inquiring mind. Is it any wonder that we have so many " yes-men " amongst us?

CHAPTER XVIII

SEX-RELATIONS IN THE LIGHT OF OCCULTISM

ONE thing the Ageless Wisdom makes us see is that sex is not the all-important thing that so many people take it to be. The Divine Ego in every one of us is sexless, a truth that Christ enunciated when He said that in heaven we neither marry nor are given in marriage. Though in the subtler worlds after death we still bear a glorified likeness to the body we wore on earth, sex-congress as known here does not exist there.

In coming back to the earth, the soul does not always take a body of the same sex as the last life. The general rule is that we go through a series of incarnations on one side of life, and then change to a series on the other, though it is on record that one great Adept has never in all his long series of incarnations been a woman. The sex-differentiation persists through both the psychic and physical bodies, so that woman has a totally different mental and emotional outlook from, though complementary to, man.

The two channel the dual forces of the universe, which may be described as positive and negative—the poles of the pairs of opposites between which the universe was spun. On the physical plane and in the physical body a man channels the more positive forces of life and a woman the negative. Hence man is naturally the aggressor and leader, the active arm which goes out into the world to earn for the family and to protect it. These forces flow pre-eminently through the bony and muscular system. Hence the physical glory of a man lies in his strength. On the other hand a woman is more "within", the queen and ruler of the home. She tends to be more "conservative" than her husband. I have often thought, watching little boys and girls, that boys channel Shiva, the Destroyer, and girls Vishnu, the Preserver. The less positive forces follow largely the line of the glands and nerves. On the whole women have a more sensitive nervous organization than men.

But on the inner emotional plane the position becomes reversed. At the emotional levels a woman is more positive and a man more negative. He is easily led by his emotions and passions. His emotions are often simpler than a woman's. The positive force of her feelings inclines the undisciplined, unevolved woman to possessiveness, jealousy and hysteria.

On the mental plane the position is again reversed. Mentally men are more positive and definite, better generally at direction, larger in outlook than many women, and incorrigibly wedded to "facts". A woman's mind is more coloured by her emotions, more personal, more occupied with details.

On the more spiritual, intuitive plane woman again leads. The famed intuition of woman, which in the lesser developed types shows as a certain shrewdness, has some truth behind it. Hence also the well-known tendency towards religion and mysticism in women. Lord Byron spoke truly when he wrote that love was of man's life a thing apart, but was woman's whole existence. Thus the two sexes are not superior or inferior to each other, but complementary, and the viewpoint of each is equally valuable though different.

The tremendous and varied sex-problems of the world are due to the exaggeration of one factor, the mind in man, with its powers of memory and anticipation and uncontrolled imagination. This today is aided and abetted on all sides by commerce in its books, pictures and advertisements appealing directly to this side of humanity. This enormous stimulation of the imagination has placed man in a different category from the animal kingdom. With the animal world the sex-urge is periodic, and quiescent at other times. With man it is perpetually present.

H. P. Blavatsky, in *The Secret Doctrine*, says that this accentuation of the sex-urge in man and its consequent abuse is the true hereditary cause of most human physical ills.

> Creative powers in man were the gift of Divine Wisdom, not the result of sin. . . . Nor was the Curse of Karma called down upon them for seeking *natural* union, as all the mindless animal-world does in its proper season; but, for abusing the creative power, for desecrating the divine gift, and wasting the

life essence for no purpose except bestial personal gratification. . . .

In the beginning conception was as easy for woman as it was for the animal creation. Nature had never intended that woman should bring forth her young "in sorrow". . . For the seed of woman, or lust, *bruised the head* of the seed of *the fruit of wisdom and knowledge*, by turning the holy mystery of procreation into animal gratification; hence the Law of Karma "bruised the *heel*" of the Atlantean Race, by gradually changing physiologically, morally, physically, and mentally, the whole nature of the Fourth Race of mankind, until from being the healthy king of animal creation in the Third Race, man became in the Fifth, our Race, a helpless, scrofulous being, and has now become the wealthiest heir on the Globe to constitutional and hereditary diseases, the most consciously and intelligently bestial of all animals!

This is the real Curse from the physiological standpoint . . . With the arts the "fire" (i.e. mind power) received has turned into the greatest curse; the animal element, and *consciousness* of its possession, has changed periodical instinct into chronic animalism and sensuality. It is this which hangs over humanity like a heavy funeral pall. (*S. D.*, II. 428-30)

The uncontrolled imagination accentuates the sex-urge. Perhaps we have here a key to what is called sublimation, and also a clear indication that an unsophisticated, natural approach to the question, which will avoid the arousing of unhealthy curiosity and morbid secrecy, is right.

We should also recognize that the "creative" force which operates on the physical plane in sexual union has many variants, and in some form is active at every level of consciousness and its corresponding degree of matter. Thus mental discovery and inquiry are a form of it; worship, loving appreciation and generous sharing are part of it; the making of things by hand, and all the arts, are variants. Here we can see the supreme value of religious aspiration, hero-worship, self-inspired discoveries and explorations of all sorts, human friends, animal friends and "hobbies" of all kinds, in dealing with problems of sex. A boy or girl who is allowed to discover, to make friends, to become interested in all sorts of physical plane activities, such as gardening, carpentry, riding, swimming, even stamp-collecting, will not be likely to suffer unduly from "sex-problems", despite the bad heredity of all of us. So many problems are the result of boredom, and lack of healthy, happy contacts and occupations.

There is also an "art of love" in sexual approach which far too many people are utterly ignorant of—in this case being less intelligent than the animal kingdom, and some primitive peoples. Suffice it to say that it includes delicacy, consideration, patience, and above all, love. Distinction must here be made between pure sex-passion and true love, for they are not necessarily both present at once. Love regards the other person's happiness and rights; passion greedily grasps at its own satisfaction. Uplifted and sanctified by great and unselfish love, the sexual union can become a means of high ecstasy, of mystical union with Nature and the universe. Kathleen Windsor, in *Star Money*, rightly describes it: "Every one knows, who has had a thoroughly satisfying love affair, that at the end there is a kind of dying, a release from yourself and almost from life for a few moments, that spreads out into time and space." Could we say that a true lover can become for the beloved the "door to God"? An Egyptian Master has expressed it thus:

> Know, O Brother mine, that where a truly spiritual love seeks to consolidate itself doubly by a pure, permanent union of the two, in its earthly sense, it commits no sin, no crime in the eyes of the great Ain-Soph, for it is but the divine repetition of the Male and Female Principles—the microcosmal reflection of the first condition of Creation. On such a union angels may well smile! But they are rare, Brother mine.

And Plato wrote:

> Men have called Love Eros, because he has wings; the Gods have called him Pteros, because he has the virtue of giving wings.

We come up against the question of celibacy. All the religions have taught that celibacy is requisite for the attainment of spiritual knowledge. Celibacy is requisite at a certain stage of *psychic* development, but there is nothing "unspiritual" in the divinely ordained processes of Nature. Spiritual growth is as possible to a married man as to a celibate. Our thought about these things must be true, or their beauty and usefulness are impaired.

One last word, *Love* must sanctify sex. Love, comradeship, mutual tolerance and consideration must begin to grow from the very early days of marriage, or a future wreckage is inevitable. Happy the couple who have made enduring *friends* with each other before the days of passion begin to wane. The great psychologist Carl Jung has said the same as the spiritual teacher Krishnamurti. Writes Jung: "When there is a sexual problem it can only be solved by love." And Krishnaji says: "There is no sex problem which cannot be solved by love." So once again, in the words of the old Latin saying: *Omnia vincit amor*, "Love conquers all."

CHAPTER XIX

THE HOSTS OF THE INVISIBLE

MAN is not the only form of life evolving on this planet. A far larger and more varied form of life is evolving in the surrounding invisible worlds which never touches the physical plane at all. They include the intelligent forces behind all the phenomena of Nature, as well as mighty beings enormously in advance of man in spiritual stature and knowledge. They are *not* men, though often wearing a human appearance. As they live in the luminous, plastically responsive matter of the inner worlds, their form and radiant emanations are far more plastic and responsive than ours. The heavy consistency of physical matter has rendered ours more set and inelastic. Living always in more luminous spheres, seers who have caught sight of them have called them *devas* or "shining ones", a term used also by John Bunyan. There are so many ranks, stages and functions among them that only the merest sketch is possible.

The Deva Kingdom is meant to be the companion of and the co-operator with man; one writer has put it thus, that the Deva Kingdom provides the living warp of life and man the woof. But blindness, obtuseness and disharmony often prevent any co-operation.

One difference between Devas and men is that the Devas deal with a simple force, become in fact the embodiment of it, whilst man can deal with many at once and is therfore more complex. The Devas are simple, natural, elemental, knowing no personal pain or sorrow, and therefore having no consciousness of "sin" as man understands it. They are confined to their "Ray", or path in evolution, more than man is, who can "change his Ray", or work on several at once.

Those who are most in touch with the Deva Kingdom are persons who are simple, in close touch with Nature, such as simple peasants, and artists of all kinds. In comparison with the fluidic, responsive Deva, man is bare and prosaic. The Deva is poetic and romantic. This living, Devic warp of life is called by Emerson, "God in distribution". There are certain parts of the world, and certain ages of the world, where and when the Devic influence is more apparent. The parts of the world where it is more clearly evident are parts remote from towns, unspoilt by man, redolent of natural beauty. Among mountains, for example, there exist many mighty and majestic Devas—which may account for the awe and upliftment that many mountaineers feel. Indeed, it may be said that any natural beauty spot that is particularly "magical" owes that atmosphere to the presence of Devas. They are not very plentiful near big cities, disliking the inevitable disharmony and unrest there engendered.

The ages which show their influence the most vividly are those epochs of renaissance which produce great poets, artists, musicians. Milton detected their influence in what he called the "wood notes wild". It shows in many a folk element in music. There is a "singing quality" about them—magic, natural, original, innocent, unspoilt. It is the mark of being rooted in an art beyond all art. A Devic influence on literature produces what Matthew Arnold described as the "grand style'. Pre-eminent amongst the Deva-influenced poets was Percy Bysshe Shelley, that poet of "fire and dew". Another poet, mystic and artist who was tremendously in touch with them is William Blake. So was Coleridge in those magical poems of his, *Kubla Khan* and *The Ancient Mariner*.

Where the Devic influence is weak, a period of imitativeness, aridity, sophistication sets in. Nature is more or less unself-conscious and therefore co-operative. Man is intensely self-conscious and therefore, in early stages, selfish, obtuse, greedy, acquisitive. Only the unself-conscious and sensitive of soul can detect the underlying melody of Nature. Wrote Keats: "Heard melodies are sweet, but those unheard are sweeter." *Light on the Path* tells us to "Listen to the song of life," to look for it in our own heart, ever deeper and deeper until we find it. "There is a natural melody, an obscure fount, in every human heart . . . Life itself has speech and is never silent. And its utterance is not, as you that are deaf may suppose, a cry; it is a song." This song of Nature can sometimes be detected by the sensitive in the woods and hills and in lonely country places. It constitutes a kind of "harmony of the spheres". The writer has come across more than one person who had heard it. For example, lecturing once in Africa on this very subject, a man in the audience, come for the first time to such a lecture, joined the Society afterwards, because he had heard it when laying roads in Northern Rhodesia, and never knew till that moment what it was that he had heard.

Now to classify the vast hosts of invisible beauty that surround us, very broadly speaking, we can arrange them in three main divisions:

1. The souls of the Elements;
2. The soul of organized Nature;
3. The Higher Devas connected with man and the working of the Karmic Law.

With regard to the elements, it may be said that there is no activity without some kind of consciousness or intelligence behind it, though not necessarily like *human* intelligence. Sir Oliver Lodge once said that the "whole universe is the ever-growing garment of a transcendent God". He also pointed out that as knowledge is embodied in its knowers, so activity is the outcome of actors. We do not see the invisible life and intelligence that is behind the wind blowing, and the flowers growing, but it is there. We are in the position of a being from another planet arriving here without the ability to see men. He would then see trains running, houses going up, etc. apparently all by themselves! Dr. Annie Besant once said that even behind chemical action lay the consciousness of a "God". As H. P. Blavatsky put it: "There is no dead matter. Every last atom is alive. Every atom of substance, no matter of what plane, is in itself a Life."

The ancient alchemists considered the four elements, earth, water, air and fire, to be ensouled by four classes of "nature-spirits" whom they named gnomes, undines, sylphs and salamanders. These give their special quality to the element. Without the salamanders fire would not burn. This may provide the explanation of the well-known phenomenon of "fire-walking"; by mantram or pact the officiating priest inhibits the salamanders from acting. A Breton lady once told the writer of an event that she saw with her own eyes in the village in Brittany where she was born. One day some hay-ricks caught fire. It was too far for anyone to fetch the fire-brigade in time, so someone suggested fetching an old peasant who had the secret of putting out fire, handed down in his family for generations from father to son. The old man came and walked round the burning ricks muttering something in an unknown tongue. Immediately every flame went out.

Gnomes work in the ground, bringing about changes and transmutations in the earth. They sometimes appear above it and are caught sight of by simple-people with sharpened eyesight, for gnomes are composed of the finer, etheric side of physical matter and are not too difficult to see. Their hosts are ruled by a mighty Deva, or Angel, called Kubera in India and Vulcan in the West. A miner, who for many years kept watch in the mines at night, told the writer that he often heard the footsteps and the knocks of the gnomes.

The undines lend sparkle to the flowing water, and the sylphs direct the air-currents and build the cloud formations. The sylphs are the most highly evolved and intelligent of the elemental nature-spirits and have been known to come into contact with man and to form relationship with him.

The Christian Bible mentions these elemental spirits. In *Revelations* St. John writes that he " saw four angels standing on the four corners of the earth, holding the four winds ". (Cf. the Greek " Boreas ", etc.) He also writes that another angel came out from the altar, which had power over fire. And again: " I heard the angel of the waters say . . ." The Hebrew scholar, Maimonides, says: " Natural forces and angels are identical."

The next division is what I have named the soul of organized Nature. This means the hidden life and intelligence behind the growth of flowers and trees. The soul of the flowers, the flower-fairies, are an exceptionally lovely creation, taking somewhat the form and the colours of the flowers of which they are the guardian spirits. Says the *Bundahish*: " Every single flower is appropriate to an angel." This is the true origin of what is called spontaneous and protective variation. It means that the little fairy guardian of the flowers has what we might call a " brain-wave "; so also the fairy guardians of certain insects and small creatures bring about protective colouring and form in their charges.

These constitute the " little people " and the fairy kingdoms of primitive legend and clairvoyance. As is often the case, folklore and tradition are right. The Greeks people the woods and streams, etc. with dryads, naiads and oreads. The Celtic countries have their kelpies, leprechauns, etc. Not only primitive people catch sight of them, but sometimes also children. The writer knew a family in Donegal who had a pet leprechaun in the house. Their favourite game was to try and catch him, but they never did! She also has the photograph of a dead leprechaun which was found inside a large toadstool in Phoenix Park, Dublin; and she personally knew the two children whose photographs of "fairies" have become world-famous. How many people has she met who played with fairies when they were little children, and were sometimes punished for talking about them.

The following description of "fairies" was written to her in a letter from a stranger who had been hearing one of her radio talks in Australia:

> It was a glorious moonlight evening. Tempted by the mystery and the witchery of the stillness which lay around I went into my garden. Suddenly and silently they appeared, Nature Spirits. I stood entranced, watching them in their light, airy flight. They were about eighteen inches in length, and from their shoulders there came a beautiful shimmering radiance. This auric flow of light seemed to be downward and outward, mingling with the arms to form wings.
>
> They paused a moment in their flight, the moonlight encircled them making them appear like scintillating jewels in delicate colours of green, gold and blue, living opals. Lightly they swept over a high bank of laurels and disappeared.

Then there are the "Spirits of the Mountains", something like, though not so solid-looking, as Sir Frederick Leighton's famous picture; and there are the "Ladies of the Lakes". They often take a near-human form, but they are protean creatures and can take any form which pleases them.

Some elemental forms are of an unpleasant appearance—those which are attracted to slaughter-houses, drink-shops, etc. There is quite a good deal of truth in the old saying that "cleanliness is next to godliness", for beauty and cleanliness attract a very lovely unseen life, whilst dirt and disorder and decaying matter attract the opposite. The spirit of a tree is a very lovely thing. The writer once knew a man who loved trees and felt he could talk to them. Of all the tree kingdom the trees which like man best are the firs. Out in the great deeps, mighty sea-spirits are sometimes visible. Like the albatross they are to be found far from land.

The third great division includes beings as intelligent as and often far greater and more spiritual than man. To these we may more appropriately apply the old name of Angel, although they do not have wings. That tradition may have arisen from two facts: one, that on the subtle, radiant planes of Nature, where forces are visible and audible in sound and colour, the great Devas channel them through their own radiant plastic bodies, and to put it in the thought-words of one such: "The Higher Devas are channels of vast out-rushing forces which lend them the appearance of wings." The tradition is older than Christianity, for on the walls of an ancient Pompeian house may be seen to this day the figures of angels with wings and wearing blue halos, instead of golden ones as is customary in Christian countries. This order of Devas often comes into contact with man. They are of many and various kinds, and wear, more or less, a human appearance. There are the Gandharvas, or angels of sound, who inspire musicians, the angels of colour who influence painters, rank upon rank, right up to the great Angels of Creation who help to bring solar systems into being, when " the gods " (as it should be translated) created the heavens and the earth, " when the morning stars sang together, and all the sons of God shouted for joy ".

Among them are the angels who are concerned with the reactions of Karmic Law, sometimes of retribution as " when the angel stretched out his hand upon Jerusalem to destroy it " (*II Sam.*, 24. 16); and sometimes of deliverance as when Elisha prayed, and the Lord opened the eyes of the young man with him, and he beheld " the mountain was full of horses and chariots of fire round about Elisha ". To this category belong the famed " Angels of Mons " who were seen and described to the writer by a certain Major Cannan, later killed in action.

The idea of the " Guardian Angel " is very dear to the hearts of men, though the real Guardian Angel of each one of us is our own inner Divinity. Who does not remember the beautiful lines of Robert Browning:

> Dear and great Angel, wouldst thou only leave
> That child, when thou hast done with him, for me!

And the last lines in that lovely poem inspired by the picture of a little child being guarded by a great angel:

> O world, as God has made it! all is beauty:
> And knowing this is love, and love is duty,
> What further may be sought for or declared?

During a great earthquake, many years ago, in Taormina, Sicily, a little boy was discovered imprisoned under the ruins after many days. He declared that he had been brought food every day by a lady in shining white garments.

I have mentioned before the Great Recorders in the Book of Life, or, as India would call them, the Guardians of the Ākāshic Records. Under Their vast direction the Angels of Birth and of Death work. They formulate the plan for a man's coming body and its circumstances on earth. "Thine eyes did see my substance, yet being unperfect; and in thy book all my members were written, which in continuance were fashioned, when as yet there was none of them." (*Psalm* 139)

The Lords of Karma direct human affairs. So the Prophet Daniel writes: "This matter is by the decree of the watchers, and the demand by the word of the holy ones."

Then there are the National Devas, the guardian spirits of Nations. They sum up in themselves the higher characteristics and possibilities of the Nation. The Prophet Daniel withstood "the Prince of the Kingdom of Persia twenty-one days". And the angel said to Joshua: " As captain of the hosts of the Lord am I now come." This truth has given rise to the idea of national Patron Saints, as St. George for England, St. Andrew for Scotland, etc.

Like ourselves, the Deva Kingdom evolves upon seven main lines of growth, and just as a great Adept stands at the Head of each great Ray for men, so is there a mighty Archangel at the Head of each Ray for the Deva Kingdom. Christian tradition name these seven Archangels, the Seven Angels who " stood before God ". I know to which Ray three of these Great Ones belong; I am not certain of the other four. Thus, St. Michael, the Warrior, " He who is like unto God," is at the Head of the First Ray, the Ray of Power; St. Gabriel, the Messenger, at the Head of the Second Ray, the Ray of Love-Wisdom; and St. Raphael at the Head of the Seventh Ray, the Ray of Ceremonial Magic, and also a Ray of Healing. The Prophet Zechariah calls them: " Those seven; they are the eyes of the Lord, which run to and fro through the whole earth."

The subject of the Angelic Kingdom was taught to the Initiates in the early Christian Mysteries, or esoteric schools of the Gnostic Orders. Thus the martyred Bishop of Antioch, Ignatius, writes:

> For even I, though I am bound (for Christ) and am able to understand heavenly things, the angelic orders, and the different sorts of angels and hosts, the distinction between powers and dominions, and the diversities between thrones and authorities, the mightiness of the aeons, and the pre-eminence of the

cherubim (who know most) and the seraphim (who love most), the sublimity of the Spirit, the kingdom of the Lord, and above all the incomparable majesty of Almighty God—though I am acquainted with these things, yet am I not therefore by any means perfect, nor am I such a disciple as Paul or Peter.

All around us, unseen, are teeming hosts of vivid life. Truly John Milton wrote:

> Millions of spiritual creatures walk the earth
> Unseen, both when we wake, and when we sleep.

CHAPTER XX

THE EVOLUTION OF ANIMALS

THIS thought may surprise some readers: Is there an animal evolution? Have they a goal in life too? Quite a number of often very good but unthinking people regard the lower creations in much the same way as a young missionary next to whom I sat at meals on board. The people around noticed that I did not eat meat. They wanted to know why. Was it for health reasons? "No," I said, "but for the one simple reason that I once lived near a slaughter-yard, and could not help seeing something of what went on. I saw a young bullock break out into the street with blood streaming from a ravaged eye due to inexpert pole-axing. I saw a poor, tired sheep, whose legs simply doubled up under her with fatigue, being kicked along like a football by the drover. I do not blame the drover. It was his business to get the sheep there somehow." "Oh! don't tell us any horrors!" the table ejaculated. (They could not hear horrors, but they could enjoy eating the result of the horrors.) Then the young missionary looked up sweetly from her plate. "But, my dear Miss Codd," she said, "what did our Lord make the animals *for*?"

There you are! Quite good people think that the animal kingdom was made for us to kill, abuse, exploit, decimate merely for the joy of "hunting". I am glad the State of Denmark has prohibited hunting. It is called "sport". Is it sport for the animal concerned, or for its young left to starve after its death? Sport is supposed to mean a friendly contest between equals. Is a murderous contest between a man and an animal sport?

Because of the horrors of the trappists' work, I gave up wearing furs long years ago. Once, waiting in a dentist's parlour, I took up a paper called the *Draper's Journal*, and this is what I read: "The vanity of woman, plus the greed of man, has almost entirely decimated the wild life of the world." And what a loss! Man is beginning to discover that, and so now forms wild game reserves. I once visited the famous Game Reserve in S. Africa, where the animals do not run away from one because they have no fear, and never shall I forget the aching sense of loss that came over me when I left the Reserve and came back to a world devoid of so much wild life. There is an abounding vitality in the near proximity of wild life.

The loving heart of a Saint is friends with all that lives. St. Francis preached to "his little sisters, the birds". The mystic poet, William Blake, wrote:

> How do you know but every bird that cuts the airy way,
> Is an immense world of delight, closed by your senses five?

I know more than one hunter who has exchanged the gun for the camera.

All the kingdoms of Nature have their goal and their way of growth. The Divine Life is in all of them, unfolding in each a further and higher power. As says an old Sufi mystic:

> God sleeps in the mineral, dreams in the plant and tree, begins to awake in the animal, becomes self-conscious in man. When did I ever grow less by dying? Next time I shall die from the man that I may grow the wings of an angel. From the angel, too, must I seek advance, for all things shall perish save His Face.

The kingdoms of Nature follow the same Law of Unfoldment as takes place in the life of a child. The first thing a baby evidences is intense activity; so do puppies and kittens. Unseen by mortal eyes, the mineral kingdom in which Life is most closely " cribbed, cabined and confined ", is yet incredibly " alive ". In all the universe there is no such thing as " dead matter ". After a millennial of ages in the mineral kingdom, the Life-Wave passes on into the vegetable kingdom, and here it begins to " feel ". Not that it *knows* it feels. That is a different thing. Remember the flowers that turn and open to the sun, the sensitive leaves that curl up when touched. I once heard a fascinating lecture by the great Indian scientist, Sir Jagadis Chandra Bose, on the " Nervous System in Plants ". He had invented a machine which registered a plant's response to the surrounding forces of Nature. He found that a sheltered plant did not produce such an organized nervous system as one exposed to the winds and storms of life—a moral for all of us!

Coming into the animal kingdom, life not only grows and feels but begins to think. Indeed, some animals in their little way think very clearly and keenly as all who love and watch animals have observed. If it be objected that there is no " missing link " to prove this gradual ascent through the kingdoms of Nature it must be replied that we can only observe segments of the kingdoms on this planet. The whole Life-Wave includes many planets, interior and exterior.

Now there is a fundamental difference between man and the lower kingdoms and between man and the animal kingdom. All the lower kingdoms below man, including even the animal kingdom, are hardly *self*-conscious. They are conscious after their fashion, but not self-conscious. They are moved by a hidden, corporate intelligence which we may designate a Group-Soul. The great naturalist, Eugene Marais, without the aid of any occult knowledge discovered the existence of this corporate intelligence in his studies of the life of the white ant. " We may term this phenomenon," he writes, " the ' group psyche or soul '."

This is the origin of animal instinct, as the herd instinct which, when one sheep jumps through a hedge, causes all the others to follow him. A friend of mine, who was brought up on a ranch in America, was taught by Red Indians how to hypnotize animals. One day he hypnotized a horse on his father's ranch to persuade it that it was lame in the left fore-leg, and, to his astonishment, found every other horse there going lame!

Eugene Marais also notices something else, that the higher the animal, the more individual memory they seem to possess. The hidden truth behind that is that all share group-souls. After death an animal's individual consciousness and experiences are absorbed by the group-soul and tend to add to the instinctive knowledge of the group. Witness, for instance, the way the group-soul of horses has become accustomed to motor cars, and how certain wild animals are now wary of a gun.

The lower small animals, such as bees and butterflies and ants, share a common group-soul in enormous numbers. They are also in contact with the lower orders of Devic intelligences who help them to bring about "protective variation", etc. But the greater the growth and intelligence of the species, the fewer the numbers sharing one group-soul, until, among the higher mammals, quite a small number share life together.

These group-souls are the origin of species, and when a new sub-species arises, it means a cleavage in the group-soul brought about by very differing experiences. Thus, life ascends the scale until it reaches what we call the "domestic animals", those brought into contact with man. Why are they brought into contact with man? For us to eat, exploit and abuse? No, far otherwise!

I now return to the fundamental difference between even the higher animals and man. It is this: man is a trinity, possessing a body, a soul, and an immortal, undying Spirit; the animals possess bodies and souls, or psychic counterparts, which in the case of the higher animals, live for some time a separate, individual life after death, but are not yet vehicles for the incoming of a Divine Spark of Deity, hereafter to be gradually shaped and redeemed by Him.

Years ago I used to broadcast on these subjects in Australia, and one of my listeners asked a Catholic priest whether it was true that animals "had souls", as I had stated. His reply was that they had no souls and therefore cruelty to an animal was not a "mortal sin". On the other hand, there is the exquisite tale of Father Robert Hugh Benson about two little sparrows shot "for fun" by some boys, and how an angel took their little, quivering souls in her hands as they left their feathery bodies, and soothed them.

Animals *do* have souls, and some of them live individual lives for quite a time after death. This is even more the case with an animal that has been made a friend by man. It is to be noticed in the rapid growth of intelligence and emotional response in an animal well cared for and befriended. Certain animals head the long growth of their species. Horses have behind them a long anterior evolution from the little creature of the prehistoric ages; the domestic dog is at the head of the canine tribe; the cat leads the feline species. These animals are now in constant contact with man, for *their own sakes*, not ours.

The beautiful phenomenon now becoming possible is very difficult to describe. It can only happen with particularly favoured specimens of four animal species: the horse, the dog, the cat, and the monkey. These lead the animal evolutionary life. Contact with man sharpens their individual intelligence; when loved and befriended, their emotional response increases. This is more easily observed in the case of a horse or a dog, the particular "friends of man".

Take a noble dog, whose master is truly his friend and who is himself a noble man. The continual companionship of the greater and higher life with the smaller, the continual play of the more highly evolved aura of the man upon the less evolved soul of the dog, brings about sometimes a remarkable heightening and expansion of the dog's mental and emotional faculties. It is a very rare happening, demanding such perfect conditions, but it *may* happen that the dog's mind and heart have so transcended the normal orbit of his kind that the attention of the waiting Deva hosts is attracted and they put a Divine Spark, waiting to commence its great evolutionary journey, into contact with that advancing animal soul, and thus, before he quits his animal body for the last time, he has already become a man, attached to an immortal Spirit. He will not reincarnate as a human being on this planet; the door is closed; but he will upon another, and it may well be that by that time his master will have reached Adeptship

—the Superhuman Kingdom. But the bond of love and friendship thus formed can never be broken, and what was a bond of friendship between a noble man and a noble animal becomes the precious bond between the Master and His disciple. In the eighteenth century, John Wesley glimpsed this truth and said:

> What if it should please the all-wise, the all-gracious Creator, to raise the animals higher in the scale of being? What if it should please Him, when He makes us "equal to the angels", to make them what we are now, capable of God; capable of knowing, and loving, and enjoying the Author of their being?

Such is the wonderful possibility at the apex of the animal evolution. How untrue that they have no goal, and were made for man! All Life is One, glorious and beautiful in meaning and purpose, and when we glimpse that ever so faintly, we begin to befriend, try to understand, co-operate with all living things, and cease to exploit, destroy, or imprison them ignorantly. The tender heart of William Blake wrote:

> A Robin Redbreast in a Cage
> Puts all Heaven in a Rage,
> A skylark wounded in the wing,
> A cherubim does cease to sing.

After all he was only echoing the sublime words of the Hebrew Prophet Isaiah:

> They shall not hurt nor destroy in all my holy mountain: for the earth shall be full of the knowledge of the Lord, as the waters cover the sea.

CHAPTER XXI

THE GREAT TYPES IN EVOLUTION

THE numbers three and seven seem to rule the universe, and so they have generally been regarded as " sacred numbers ". As stated before, life is threefold everywhere—three dimensions of space, three powers of consciousness, symbolized in the widespread doctrine of the Trinity; everything with its opposite and the relationship between. An artist, known to the writer, said that all art forms were built upon three fundamental ones, namely the straight line, the circle, and the spiral.

The number seven seems equally prevalent; the seven colours of the spectrum, the seven notes of the scale. These facts are founded upon great, underlying principles of Nature. Not only is every form of matter or plane septenary in constitution, but life through all the kingdoms of Nature evolves along seven main lines of unfoldment. These are popularly designated the " Seven Rays ":

> Those seven; they are the eyes of the Lord, which run to and fro through the whole earth. (*Zechariah*, 4. 10)

First, let us notice the broad, general, threefold division of human types. They are fairly evident, according to whether thought, emotion or activity predominates in a man's make-up. The type produces a fundamental inner idealism, for a man's ideals are founded upon that which is germane to his nature, that, in fact, which he has the inborn capacity to achieve.

These are the main three: The man of thought often develops into a scientist or philosopher, and his inner idealism pictures him as a Sage in the future. The emotional man is more likely to picture himself as a future Saviour or Saint, going about doing good. The man devoted to action, who in early stages will be likely to look down upon the other two types as "dreamers", is likely to prefer a future as Hero, Leader, Statesman.

The great figures along these lines lead the world's development. We may say that they are in the top class in the School of Life, already transcending national and sectarian boundaries, and preparing to leave the school for the higher kingdom beyond. There they will enter different classes of Adepts; those of the World Governors, World Saviours and Teachers, and World Sages or Magicians.

But the threefold classification subdivides again into seven, constituting seven main lines of development and experience. It must not be presumed that an individual belongs to one main type only, for we all have the seven great characteristics in us. It means that one is predominant, rather colouring the whole, and there is generally another next in predominance, as the keynote and sub-dominant of the musical scale.

Another fact to be noticed is that it is very difficult to tell the type in the early days of evolution. It does not begin to show clearly until the soul is approaching the higher stages, and then becomes more clearly evident to clairvoyant vision by the arrangement of colour in the psychic aura. It is as if the soul first of all receives an all-round education, and begins to " specialize " in the higher reaches.

Another truth to be remembered is that we are not bound to remain upon one particular road in evolution. We may change. This is done, though it may take several lives to accomplish completely, by industriously accentuating the qualities of the Ray to which we wish to transfer, until those qualities become predominant, and the former predominant ones take a secondary place.

We will now try to describe the main characteristics of the Seven Rays, mentioning what is known so far of the minerals, plants and animals, which are also upon the Ray. An enormous amount of research is awaited upon this subject.

Ray 1 is sometimes called the Ray of Power. To this Ray belong all those who have an inborn capacity to govern and lead. If the foreman of a gang of workmen has this quality, even in a rudimentary degree, he will be more successful than one who has it not. Such people, when well developed, are naturally strong, brave and persevering. Their minds easily work on a grand scale, rendering them rather impatient of detail. Some of them have a dramatic touch, whilst another type of " leader " is magnetic and winning.

The undeveloped type on this Ray can often be arrogant, obstinate and tyrannical, often intensely autocratic, and will develop into the higher type by learning patience, humility and compassion.

The great Adept who is the Chohan or Lord of this Ray for men is the one known in Theosophical literature as the Master Morya. He has been a ruling Raja in India, and is the future " Manu " or Leader of the coming Sixth Root Race.

The jewel upon this Ray is the diamond, and its " colour " is white, from which other colours are partial variants, symbolizing the fact that a soul must pass on to this fundamental Ray to leave the " Ring-Pass-not " of this solar system.

The religion and civilization predominantly influenced by this Ray is that of ancient India. Its method of dealing with things, and also of healing, is by sheer Will, recognizing no obstacles. The Head of this Ray in the Deva Kingdom is the Archangel Michael, the " Warrior " of God.

Ray 2 is that of Love-Wisdom. To that Ray belong all the great Saviours and Teachers of the world. It has a natural intuitional wisdom developed through love. Its strength lies in its powers of endurance and its natural serenity. In the undeveloped stages it can become rigid, aloof and indolent, and therefore has to cultivate energy and understanding.

The jewel upon this Ray is the sapphire, the " holy jewel ", and the colour is blue. Certain trees are upon this Ray, as the tulsi tree of India, and all the lily species. Passing on into the animal kingdom, they become the elephant tribe, the most sagacious of all beasts. Among the Devas, the Head of this Ray is the Archangel Gabriel, the " Messenger " of God, generally depicted as bearing an " annunciation lily " in his hand. It largely influenced the religion of Buddhism.

Ray 3 is more philosophic and is connected with the higher or metaphysical mind. It has large-minded, gracious characteristics, is generally lucid in its mental conceptions, though given to pride and cynicism in its lower stages of development. The jewel is the emerald, and the colour green.

Very often upon this Ray are to be found such idealistic lovers as Dante and Beatrice. The love-power of Ray 1 is intense for some, of Ray 2, more spread over humanity.

Ray 3 influenced the astrology of Chaldea, and to this Ray belong the rose species and the deer.

Ray 4 is the Ray of Balance, the turning between the higher aspects of man and his more personal attributes. It is also sometimes called the Ray of Harmony and Beauty, and quite a number of artists are upon this Ray. Very often such people have great physical magnetism and vivacity, as well as courageous and affectionate natures. The undeveloped type can be very turbulent and lazy. Nearly all of them swing between the poles of great exaltation and corresponding depression. They need to develop self-control. They also often possess a certain grace of movement, and this can be seen in the animals on this Ray, the feline tribe.

Ray 5 depicts the concrete, factual mind, and is often the Ray of the born scientist with his passion for detailed knowledge and patient accuracy. Such people are independent-minded and inherently just, but can be also narrow-minded and hard. " Breadth " is their goal. The jewel is the topaz, and the colour is yellow.

Ray 6 corresponds to the fluctuating emotional body and is pre-eminently the Ray of the religious devotee and the born " hero-worshipper ". Reverence, gentleness and sincerity characterize the better developed members of this type. The undeveloped can become very superstitious, bigoted and sectarian. They must learn tolerance. Because of its connection with the personal feelings and passions, purity is its ideal, and to it belong certain forms of asceticism. The form of devotion is an intense love of God in personal form, generally in the Person of a great Mediator, as the Lord Christ, and their way is the way of prayer and self-surrender.

The jewel of this Ray is the glowing ruby and the colour is red. The animal upon this Ray is easily detected—the slavishly devoted, hero-worshipping dog!

A religion and civilization which was tremendously influenced by this Ray was the Christian, the religion pre-eminently of love and devotion, and producing, at its peak period, a wonderful galaxy of great Christian

Saints. The world-influence of this Ray is waning now, and its successor, *Ray 7*, is mounting in the scale of influence. This is the Ray of ordered service or ceremonial, invoking upon the inner side of life the help of the great Deva or Angelic Kingdom. It has two aspects, according to a person's mental make-up. One is devoted to symbolism and allegory, seeing symbols and glyphs everywhere, and learning through them; the other has an innate awareness of the wielding and channelling of interior power through occultly constructed ceremonial, and hence also in all magical workings.

It produces in its devotees a sense of order, harmony and grace, but the undeveloped members of this type can evince a surprising ultra-orthodoxy, conceit and shallowness. Unity and love is their goal. The jewel is the amethyst, and the colour violet. Through co-operative work with the Deva Kingdom this Ray is also to a large extent a " healing " Ray, and has, as its Angel Guardian, the Archangel Raphael. Under its influence are all true ceremonial movements, the doyen of which is the Adept who once was a Hungarian Prince and who now is the Adept Overseer of modern civilization in Europe and America.

It will be seen that all this information is very partial and incomplete, but it is interesting and provocative of thought. Perhaps its greatest value at present lies in the impression it can give one of the wonderful diversity in unity of the universe, or, to put it in familiar parlance, how it " takes all sorts to make a world ".

We should be very careful in trying to set ourselves, or others, into any of these niches, so partially described. Let it suffice to help create for us a picture of the infinite variety of life, with all its multifarious relationships and correspondences.

CHAPTER XXII

THE ADEPTS—THE MASTERS OF THE WISDOM

IF evolution is true, perfected men are a logical necessity. For untold ages, in the history of this planet, great master-minds, sages and adepts have garnered a deep knowledge about man and his method of evolution and have handed it on from one generation to another; and now, in these modern days, they have lifted a tiny corner of the veil which screens this tremendous knowledge, and given us, through their pupils, an outline of the universal principles which govern all life.

This knowledge and wisdom await all of us in time. Life by life we grow in soul stature, and there will come a time when life, either on this side or the other, will hold no more to teach us. Then we shall be nearing the stature of a Perfect Man, an Adept of knowledge, power, compassion and love. Some are even now nearer than others, but some time, somewhere, all will reach it, for we all have the germ of perfectability in us. " Somewhere the weariest river winds safely to the sea." For man is a god in the making, and one day he will come to the fullness and the stature of his diviner Self.

When that Superhuman Kingdom is reached, several paths of development open out before the Adept, some of them leading far away from earth. But one that may be chosen is to remain for untold millennia here on this earth and its surrounding inner realms, forming part of the great hierarchy of the Freed Men who guard and help ascending humanity, so far as the Great Law permits.

There are many grades and many classes of Adepts engaged in this work, and even before he reaches the Path of Discipleship a man is often marked out by his inborn characteristics for one or the other grade or class. There are the Adepts whom we might describe as World-Governors—leaders and guardians of evolving races or types of humanity. They are always concerned with methods of government, emigrations, the rise and fall of nations, and so forth on that line. Where possible they inspire great leaders and statesmen, like the " spirit of the Lord " which rested upon King Saul in his better days. Moses and the Indian Manu are typical examples.

Another class, better known because great Adepts of this type appear before men sometimes on the physical plane, is of the great religious Teachers and founders of religions such as have appeared at intervals in the past. They are concerned, not so much with racial types and systems of government, but with the inner growth of man as an intelligence and soul. Let us call it the Department of Religion and Education.

Still another class is occupied with great scientific discoveries and progress in the fields of sociology, human relationships, art, medicine, etc. It is almost as if, graduating from the School of Life, some return as Professors in the School. It is a sacrifice for a Perfected Man thus to return to physical encasement and life, but for our sake, to be nearer to us here, he "accepts the woes of birth".

What is he like, a perfected man, who still retains a physical body? I think we must try to realize that a Master of the Wisdom is not a "god" to be worshipped and propitiated, but a man like ourselves, albeit a very splendid, spiritual and noble man. Even the first President of the Theosophical Society, Colonel H. S. Olcott, having come through Spiritualism and having met Madame Blavatsky at the Eddy Homestead, for some time persisted in regarding the Adepts as a kind of "spirit guides". One day a Master wrote to him:

> The time is come to let you know who I am. I am not a disembodied spirit, Brother, I am a living man; gifted with such powers by our Lodge as are in store for yourself some day. I cannot be with you otherwise than in spirit, for thousands of miles separate us at present.

A great disciple of One such once described in the writer's hearing what a Master of the Wisdom would look like on the physical plane. I will quote his words:

> Suppose a Master of the Wisdom walked into this room, which is just possible though not likely, you would not at first see any particular difference from ourselves, for the Master is still man. But you would see a very distinguished and splendid looking man, having a perfectly healthy body, for, not only does the Master know and obey the laws of health better

than we do, but he also has no evil karma from the past which would bring him disease or deformity.

Perhaps the greatest difference would be in the expression of his eyes, and there you would see three very important things. First of all, you would observe in them a look of very high purpose which lends them a far-away, starry look. For the Master's interior thoughts are always centred upon great, impersonal issues, never on petty things concerned only with himself. Indeed, he never thinks of himself at all.

Then you would also see a great benevolence, for the Master is pre-eminently kind, compassionate, and understanding. And do not think there will never be a glint of humour there! All Adepts have a great sense of humour. They would never laugh *at* anyone, but they might easily poke gentle fun at a pupil who was taking himself too seriously.

And lastly there would be an expression of deep and enduring peace, for an Adept never worries or fusses, not even about us. He knows that in the end all will be well for every one, and has no fear of the ultimate result, but in his deep kindliness he would like us to come along more quickly, and not pile up so much trouble for ourselves.

This Divinely Motherly attitude of some Adepts is described in very sweet and simple terms by the Lord Buddha. He said one day to His bhikkhus or monks:

I will show you how the Tathāgata looks on humanity. He anxiously watches over his children and with loving care helps them to see the light. When a hen has ten or twelve eggs, over which she has properly brooded, the wish arises in her heart, "Oh that my little chickens would break open the egg-shell with their claws, or with their beaks, and come forth into the light in safety!" Yet all the while those little chickens are sure to break the egg-shell and will come forth into the light in safety, but in her mother's heart she would like them to come sooner.

How like the compassionate words of the Lord Christ when He mourned over Jerusalem and cried:

> How often would I have gathered thy children together, even as a hen gathereth her chickens under her wings, and ye would not! . . . If thou hadst known, even thou, at least in this thy day, the things which belong unto thy peace! but now they are hid from thine eyes.

I can imagine a Master of the Wisdom feeling that, when the ghastliness of the World War broke upon us. But although upon the physical plane They are still men, on the inner planes Their development is enormously in advance of and transcends our own. Some idea of the tremendous difference can be indicated thus. The ordinary civilized man has pretty well reached the limits of his physical development. In the upper ranks of humanity he also possesses a well-organized psychic body capable of conscious, independent existence apart from the body during sleep. The mental powers are still fairly rudimentary in many people, but in some glimmerings of the spiritual Self may be distinguished. Besides, the link between the different states of consciousness in the developed sheaths of the Self is not yet formed. In the case of the Adept, all planes are open to Him, His consciousness is fully awake on all of them, the vehicles of that consciousness are fully developed, and the links between them formed and active, so that the waking consciousness of the Adept is playing up and down between them all the time. He is a " whole " man, body, soul and Spirit.

How does an Adept work to help us? Why, for instance, did He not stop the World War? Because the Laws of the Great Brotherhood of Life to which He belongs are adamant and never broken, and one law is that once any intelligence starts a cause operating it must be allowed to run its course. In the words of *The Voice of the Silence*: " Teach to eschew all causes; the ripple of effect, as the great tidal wave, thou shalt let run its course." An Adept once asked the Vice-President of the Theosophical Society to get his people to understand that They were the agents and not the arbiters of Karma. How would humanity learn, except by the exact result of their corporate short-sightedness, ignorance and greed?

But where He can, and when He can, the Master always helps. These are a few of the ways. On a high plane of subtle forms, each body or group of men which works on earth for human good, such as the religions and humanitarian reform bodies, forms one organism or body, so to say, and every individual belonging to that movement is a cell in this body or organism. Every such body becomes a chalice with its own special life which all belonging to it share. Into such chalices the Master pours the wine of grace and inspiration.

On the mental plane, the Master makes special thought-forms which may be picked up by human minds aspiring along the same line and which then become inspiration and enlightenment. He also casts helpful thought into the minds of great leaders, writers, statesmen and preachers. To those who meditate and pray He often gives help and comfort. He fills the "heaven-world" of countless people with love and bliss. He aids the newly dead. He teaches his younger disciples. In a Master's own words:

> How few are they who can know anything about us . . . We never try to subject to ourselves the will of another. At favourable times we let loose elevating influences which strike various persons in various ways.

On the physical plane the least of Their work is done, since work on the subtler planes is infinitely more effective, but They watch the tendencies of events, neutralizing, as far as the Law permits, evil currents, by a constant balancing of forces. They work with the Angel Guardians of Nations, guiding spiritual forces as we guide material ones. They choose and reject Their leading agents among men in the drama of life, influencing human councils when they can, and supplying needful impulses in a right direction.

The Voice of the Silence names them the "Guardian Wall," and speaks of them thus:

> Self-doomed to live through future Kalpas (ages), unthanked and unperceived by men; wedged as a stone with countless other stones which form the Guardian Wall . . . Built by the hands of many Masters of compassion, raised by their tortures, by their blood cemented, it shields mankind, since man

is man, protecting it from further and far greater misery and sorrow.

They are indeed our Elder Brothers, in whom is born that supernal consciousness which we all share in the depths of our being. St. Paul thus well describes one of the greatest of all Masters, the Lord Christ, who now is the spiritual Guide and Teacher of all men without exception:

> Though he were a Son, [as we all are fundamentally] yet learned he obedience by the things which he suffered; [in other lives, surely]. And being made perfect, [as we all will, one day] he became the author of eternal salvation unto all them that obey him; called of God an high priest after the order of Melchisedec.

What is the "order of Melchisedec"? Surely the same as what the Buddhists call the "succession of Buddhas or Enlightened Ones", and what Hinduism calls the "Jagat Gurus" or World Teachers. The world has never been left without divine guidance and help, especially in the persons of its Elder Brethren made manifest on earth. An ancient occult record has this truth in lovely words:

> There is a spiritual dynasty whose throne is never vacant, whose splendour never fails; its members form a golden chain whose links can never be torn asunder; for they draw back the world to God from whom it came.

And the poet Tennyson says:

> For so the whole round earth is every way
> Bound by gold chains about the feet of God.

CHAPTER XXIII

THE WAY TO THE MASTERS OF THE WISDOM

WHEN so lovely a truth as the constant presence and care of Elder Brothers dawns on us, it may be that in the hearts of some there will arise an over-mastering impulse to seek Them if haply we may find Them. Can They be approached and found? Yes, but some have made the mistake of seeking to find Them first upon the physical plane, taking dangerous journeys into Tibet, for example, where some of Them are said to reside. We need not go to the far East to find Them. They can be found here and now, in the realms of the soul and Spirit, by the man who has the right attitude and motive for the search, and whose *karma is ripe* for this. I must put this last in, for that is one necessity the Master may not overlook, and it is one that has inevitably been led up to by a sequence of events in the past. Only the Adept knows the long past and the future possibilities of each aspirant. No one else can possibly judge that upon the physical plane.

So let us leave that entirely in the hands of the Master of the Wisdom, and concern ourselves solely with what *is* in our power, our own inner attitude and motive. Is it pure? That is, is it completely free of any desire for personal comfort, assurance, prestige or power? These are entirely human, nor should we blame ourselves for possessing them in common with all humanity, but as long as they constitute the main motive, our soul is not speaking with a voice that can be heard in the Master's world.

All the occult scriptures warn us of this. Says *Light on the Path*: " Seek out the way . . . Yet pause and consider awhile. Is it the way you desire, or is it that there is a dim perspective in your visions of great heights to be scaled by yourself, of a great future for you to compass? Be warned. The way is to be sought for its own sake, not with regard to your feet that shall tread it."

Great intellect, useful as it is, like human notoriety does not weigh in this world of the True. The Master K. H. wrote to Mr. Sinnett: " *Nothing* draws us to any outsider save his evolving spirituality. He may be a Bacon or an Aristotle in knowledge, and still not even make his current felt a feather's weight by us." Mrs. Besant once put it in these words: " It is your purified heart, and not your well-filled head, that draws you to the Master's feet." In fact the voice that " can speak in the presence of the Masters " is a man's dawning spirituality, which in itself must not be misunderstood.

" Spirituality " is often confused with two common phenomena which have nothing necessarily to do with it. Sometimes it is confused with piety, more often pietosity. It is possible to be intensely pious without an ounce of spirituality. Then, again, in these days when there is so much interest in psychic matters, it is sometimes confounded with psychic powers. Although delicate and precise psychic powers are often the concomitant of developed spirituality, it is not invariably so, and the majority of untrained psychics in this world have either the primitive forms which they share with primitive peoples and animals and which disappears with the development of the intellectual faculties, or they have brought over a certain sensitivity from a past life spent as a seer or vestal virgin in a temple of that past. There is nothing inherently " spiritual " in viewing the phenomena of the psychic plane than there is in contemplating the objects and events of the physical world.

What then is spirituality? Mrs. Besant defines it as the " intuitive perception of the unity of all life ". Professor Radhakrishnan described it as the recognition of the fact that God is Life. It certainly is a dawning perception of the unity *and* divinity of all Life. We may best recognize it by its fruits in daily life, well set forth by St. Paul: " The fruit of the Spirit is love, joy, peace, long-suffering, gentleness, goodness, faith." Not a negative goodness, faultless because untried. But an intelligent, unselfish, whole-hearted affection for one's fellow-men and a desire to do all one can to help and inspire them without any distinctions. As an Adept once wrote: " Mere goodness is not enough."

All occult scriptures agree upon the first step: charity, love, goodwill, or as the teacher Patanjali puts it, *Ahimsa*, harmlessness. *The Voice of the Silence* says: " To live to benefit mankind is the first step." And a Master writes: " A man who places not the good of mankind above his own good is not worthy of becoming our *chela* (disciple)—he is not worthy of becoming higher in knowledge than his neighbour." Or as this same Master puts it in another letter: " You must live for other men and with them, not for or with yourself." The one obstacle which stands in the way of acquiring spiritual knowledge, the knowledge of our own Divinity, of conscious union with the Eternal Life and Love and Wisdom, and with the Master of the Wisdom to whom we aspire, is the carapace of selfhood, of separation, of " me " and " mine ". That sense of mine which was for many lives a necessary protection must be broken, that the shining, divine life may be set free, and it sometimes takes many lives to do it.

This is true Occultism, the real way to the Master's feet. H. P. Blavatsky wrote: " True Occultism is the Great Renunciation of Self, unconditionally and absolutely, in thought as in action. Not for himself but for the world he lives . . . It is impossible to employ *Spiritual* forces if there is the slightest tinge of selfishness remaining in the operator. The powers and forces of Spirit lend themselves only to the pure in heart—and this is Divine Magic."

Let us all begin to practise a *little* self-denial, less preoccupation with personal and petty desires, so that one day may come into our being here that *greater* Self, who is always a constant and unseen Blessing to all that lives.

Then, the second step, says *The Voice of the Silence*, is to "practise the six glorious virtues". These are often translated: charity, morality, patience, energy, contemplation and wisdom. They are to be compared with the Noble Eightfold Path of the Lord Buddha, and the Eight Beatitudes of the Lord Christ.

The following are the words of H. P. Blavatsky: "Meditation, abstinence in all, the observation of moral duties, good deeds and kind words, gentle thoughts, good-will to all and entire oblivion of self, are the most efficacious means of obtaining knowledge and preparing for the reception of the higher wisdom."

The following, too, is the advice of a Master to an aspirant who was already in touch with Him: "How can you know the real from the unreal, the true from the false? Only by self-development. How to get that? By first carefully guarding yourself against the causes of self-deception. And this you can do by spending a certain fixed hour or hours each day all alone in self-contemplation, writing, reading, the purification of your motives, the study and correction of your faults, the planning of your work in the external life. . . . Little by little your sight will clear, you will find the mists pass away, your interior faculties strengthen, your attraction toward us gain force, and certainty replace doubts."

Take thought, take little quiet moments when you dream, soar, aspire, acquire a delicate perception of the spiritual value of all things, and discern with the eye of faith the world of love and strength and wisdom which belongs to the eternal foundations of life. The Master will know our thoughts of Him. How could He do otherwise? He wrote to an aspirant: "I have watched your many thoughts. I have watched their silent evolution and the yearnings of your inner soul." And in gradual and unseen ways He will draw us ever nearer to Himself. "Draw nigh to God," wrote St. James, "and He will draw nigh to you." And the Master K. H. once wrote to Mr. Sinnett: "I can come nearer to you, but you must draw me by a purified heart and a rapidly developing will."

What is the will? It is not selfishly demanding what we want. To my mind it is the steady direction in which a man's soul is held, and the ancient teacher Patanjali says a similar thing: "The right use of the will is the constant endeavour to stand in spiritual being."

And the joy of the finding! How great and pure and true a friend is a Master of the Wisdom, one whose word is His bond, whose patience and compassion never falters, whose love and co-operation may be gained by true love and unfaltering service of our fellow-men. The intuition of a poet has glimpsed it. In Robert Browning's *Saul* occurs these wonderful lines:

> 'Tis the weakness in strength that I cry for; my
> flesh that I seek

In the Godhead! I seek and I find it.
O Saul, it shall be
A Face like my face that receives thee; a Man like to me
Thou shalt love and be loved by, for ever! A Hand like this hand
Shall throw open the gates of new life to thee!

And again in the *The Ring and the Book*:

Through such souls alone
God stooping shows sufficient of His light
For us i' the dark to rise by. And I rise.

We may always know the true aspirant. Nothing daunts him, nothing depresses him. He has all the patience of eternity, the never-ceasing will to serve. He asks nothing either of heaven or earth, wholly content with what comes, seeking only to do the eternal Will coming to him through the Master of his heart's desire. And the true disciple is also to be known by certain signs: he never makes claims to exterior or interior prestige. He never takes from others but seeks to give all that is his. He does not dogmatize, or seek to impose his will, ideas or advice upon others, yet his ear is ever ready to listen to another's trouble or bewilderment.

This subject is so great in extent, so deeply important in its meaning and effects, that it cannot be really dealt with in one short chapter in a book, so the writer hopes to follow this volume with another one devoted exclusively to the subject of discipleship and the inner life.

Meanwhile she would like to close this chapter with again some words of H. P. Blavatsky:

> To those dedicated to the Higher Life, keep ever in mind the consciousness that though you see no Master by your bedside, nor hear one audible whisper in the silence of the still night, yet the Holy Power is about you, the Holy Light is shining into your hour of spiritual need and aspirations.

CHAPTER XXIV

YOGA—WHAT IS IT?

THERE is a rapidly increasing interest all over the world today in the subject of " Yoga ". Schools of Yoga are springing up everywhere, as well as Institutes headed by Eastern Swamis, and mystical and meditative movements after the manner of Gerald Heard, one-time scientist, and Paul Brunton, now a leading figure in these matters. A remark of an Adept made more than seventy years ago is now clearly evidenced on all hands. " A wave of mysticism," He said, " is sweeping over Europe." It is sweeping over the world now and is a presage of new and happier things to come.

The movement gathers momentum unceasingly, and for the most part outside the orthodox Churches. The consciousness of the coming humanity is turning from the idea of God Transcendent, outside His universe, to God Immanent, within and with His world, and most of all, where the Christ told us the kingdom of Heaven lay, namely in the mysterious and glorious depths of man's immortal being. God is first to be found within, and then He will be found everywhere without as well.

The Eastern Sages have always known this, and have, through long ages, perfected a technique, which includes the whole of man's being and powers. It were well to begin with defining the meaning of the word *Yoga*. It is a Sanskrit word meaning "union", and from it we derive the English word "yoke". Union of what? The sages tell us it is conscious union of the awakened Spirit in man with the Eternal Spirit of the universe. Christian mystical terminology would call it "Union with God".

For this is the great possibility which belongs to man alone—and in this he is above the lower kingdoms—that he has a hidden faculty of knowing God, of coming face to face with the Heart of the Universe. This is because, deep within, he shares that supernal Life, and is for ever the Son of the Most High. "Man-spirit explains God-spirit as a drop of water explains the source from which it came."

The spiritual nature in man has its own consciousness and its own perfect knowledge. When I say that it has its own consciousness, I mean that it is a power which is neither mental nor emotional, but beyond and above both. We may use Bergson's term and name it the heavenly "intuition", which can intuitively perceive God, for God is not to be known of the physical senses, nor even of the trained mind. Let us put it in the words of an ancient Egyptian scripture:

> The soul of man is immortal, and its future is the future of a thing whose growth and splendour has no limit. The principle which gives life dwells in us,

and without us, is undying and eternally beneficent, is not heard, or seen, or smelt, but is perceived by the man who desires perception.

All through the ages, and up through all the lower kingdoms of Nature, life has been struggling towards that supreme event, "awaiting the manifestation of the Sons of God". Only in man, evolved man, is it possible, and the birth of this spiritual consciousness in him will make him more than man. St. Paul calls it "Christ in you, the hope of glory", and yearns over his people till "Christ be formed in you".

I said spiritual consciousness has its own knowledge, which is not the knowledge of mental facts. It is always in the depths of us awaiting evocation, and is the real source of the eternal hunger of the soul for Beauty, Wisdom and Love which constitute the real meaning of the word "religion", i.e. "binding together", which can never be killed, and which may also be called the "homing instinct" of the immortal Spirit in man. That wonderful Self is always there, "for Thou lovedst me before the foundation of the world", sleeping, gestating in the womb of our human nature, till the moment comes for its "birth". Hermes the Thrice Greatest thus expresses it: "This knowledge, my son, is never taught, but is of God, when He pleaseth, brought to remembrance." "For then the Soul will hear, and will remember." (*The Voice of the Silence*)

Now, it is towards the union of that awakened Divine Spirit in man with the Heart of the Universe that all true Schools of Yoga are orientated, and in the East, as I said, through immemorial ages, many teachers have evolved and perfected a great technique.

India recognizes many forms of Yoga discipline, that of posture, for example, of which the "Lotus" posture for meditation is well known. Difficult to achieve with stiff joints, it is ideal for deep meditation, for the spine is free, the body resting on the two pelvic bones, leaving complete freedom for the subtle currents which circulate in the spine. The postures and exercises of many Eastern Schools of Yoga are very beneficial to the body's health and to the calming of the nerves.

Then there is the control of the breathing to induce meditative states. This is best left alone, if without the guidance of an experienced teacher, as it is often dangerous to Western bodies. The converse can be observed. Deep meditation alters the character of the breathing, in some cases diminishing it almost to vanishing point in the state of deep ecstasy or trance called *samādhi*.

Again there is Yoga practice by the continual repetition of sacred names inducing a meditative state. Something similar is to be observed in the Christian use of the rosary.

All these simpler forms may be more or less summed up under the generic term of *Hatha Yoga*.

Different is *Rāja Yoga*, the "Kingly Yoga", which works from above downwards, and commences with the control of the mind by graduated steps of concentration, meditation and contemplation, leading to the supreme bliss of conscious union with God, called *samādhi* in the East and " ecstasy " in the West.

Eastern philosophy postulates four states of consciousness, each having its *kosha* or sheath. The first is the waking consciousness, concentrated and circumscribed, which we employ in the physical body. Then comes the dream consciousness used by the man apart from the body. Then the " deep sleep " consciousness, when the freed soul has penetrated to deeper and more glorious depths. And lastly, the *Turīya* state which belongs to the Divine Spirit in man, and is only reached by saints and Yogis.

Thus the technique of the inner life in the East means a gradual withdrawal from the outer consciousness ever more and more *within*. And here can be seen the rationale of the statement that sleep, death and meditation use the same gateway.

There are four little books of the famous ancient Indian teacher, Patanjali, which can be roughly translated thus: Book I, *The Theory and Practice of Yoga*; Book II, *The Preliminaries to Yoga*; Book III, *The Siddhis*, or Divine Powers, which may, or *may not*, develop in the illumined Yogi; Book IV, *The Isolation of the Soul*, describing the final states of union and ecstasy, which the great Neo-platonist Plotinus called " the flight of the alone to the Alone ".

Let us discuss them very briefly. The second aphorism of Book I states: " This Yoga is achieved by the control, and the cessation at will, of the modifications of the mind." The word translated " modifications " is the Sanskrit word *vritti*, which really means wave-lengths, vibration. The " wave-lengths " created by thinking are to be brought under control. Patanjali makes a distinction between the mind which plays on the brain as a musician plays on the piano, and the immortal seer who peers through the vesture of the mind. When the mind ceases to be continually distracted by the myriad preoccupations of earth, and becomes as still as a mirror lake, *then* it can reflect the glory of the diviner Self. " When this is accomplished," writes the Sage, " the Seer knows himself as he is, and stands in his own true nature."

So difficult is this to achieve by man that the disciple Arjuna, in the *Bhagavad Gita*, " deems the mind as hard to curb as the wind ". The Lord Sri Krishna gives the same answer as the sage Patanjali, that it *can* be done, by constant practice and by dispassion. The mind becomes peaceful and comes under control as the personal and emotional attachments and repulsions are diminished.

Book II describes the preliminary practices of Yoga, the necessary preparation, which are described as three:

1. *Whole-souled and ardent self-training*. This is the best way to translate the Sanskrit word *tapas* which means an ever-mounting flame, the ardent aspiration of the Soul. This will lead a man to a certain amount of asceticism, not necessarily imposed from without but seen as a necessity by himself, as a runner trains for a race discarding by degrees that which hinders, hampers, or is unnecessary.

2. *Deep thought and study.* This includes the growth of a man's own independent thought and intelligence, and the directing of that thought towards the sublime ends of meditation and contemplation. Occult study is less concerned with the amassing of facts than with the intuitive perception of principles.

3. *Absolute devotion to God, making Him the motive for all action.* This is the consecration and dedication of the life to That which is being sought, reaching finally that wonderful state described by St. Paul when he cried: "To me to live is Christ"; it is the *Karma Yoga* of the East.

Patanjali mentions some of the qualities the would-be Yogi must acquire. The following five aphorisms are so beautiful they can never be too often repeated:

1. The first quality to be acquired is *ahimsa*, perfect harmlessness, and the sage writes: "In the presence of one who has perfected harmlessness all hostility ceases." How beautiful to become a continual centre of love and peace!

2. Then he says we must be true, true all through, completely honest with ourselves, for "having become entirely true, the man's words and actions become creative and full of power". Here lies the everlasting power of true sincerity.

3. "When the desire to possess has left him, all things come to his hands." This reminds us of a saying of St. John of the Cross that to have nothing means to possess all; and also of the words of the Christ concerning the "poor in spirit".

4. " By deep thought (meditation) and study the student comes into touch with the Master or Deity of his heart's desire." Elsewhere he says that we may reach union with God " by meditating on that which is dearest to the heart ".

5. And finally, " Union is reached by making God the motive for all actions "; or, as the Curé d'Ars said to his people: " Do only what one can offer to God."

Book III describes the supernatural powers that often accompany the growth of a Yogi in grace. They sound like a fairy story or " Alice in Wonderland ", yet they are paralleled to some extent in the lives of Christian mystics. Here are some: a knowledge of the past and the future; the remembrance of past lives; insight into the mind and soul of another; contacting the cosmic spaces, far beyond the power of the largest telescope; contacting the infinitely little, far beyond the power of the strongest microscope.

These are flowers on the pathway to the Heart of the Universe. If we stay to pick them or play with them we shall not reach " Home ".

Book IV is the most difficult to understand of all, for it passes out of reach of normal conditions. In the words of St. Paul: " I knew a man in Christ . . . (whether in the body, I cannot tell; or whether out of the body, I cannot tell: God knoweth;) such an one caught up to the third heaven . . . and heard unspeakable words, which it is not lawful for a man to utter "; unable ever to express, for where can he find words or even similes, to express the unimaginable glory of that inner world? " Eye hath not seen, nor ear heard, neither have entered into the heart of man, the things which God hath prepared for them that love him."

Thus it will be seen that the ultimate aim of Yoga, either in its Eastern or Western form, is the sublime realization of the Presence of God, not merely the unfoldment of supernatural powers. The practice of true Yoga transforms the man, giving him splendid physical health, an acute and illumined intelligence, and a kindled and glowing heart. " Some form of Yoga," said the great Hungarian psychiatrist, Dr. Volgyesi, " is a necessity to the modern man, whose race is approaching the higher reaches of the mind." Dr. Alexis Carrel puts it rather differently, that " man integrates himself by meditation "; and that the health of the intelligence and affective sense, by moral discipline and spiritual development, is just as necessary as the health of the body and the prevention of infectious disease.

A man may soar to union with God without any of the deep knowledge commonly called " Occultism ". Some of the great Saints did this. They were not occultists in the generally accepted meaning of the term. But the Adept Community has in its keeping a vast store of knowledge concerning man and his method of development, his past history on this globe and his brightening future, which knowledge is obtainable nowhere else. But to be allowed to share in that knowledge demands the living of a pure, unselfish life, dedicated wholly to the service of God and man. H. P. Blavatsky gives us " The Golden Stairs ":

Behold the Truth before you: A clean life, an open mind, a pure heart, an eager intellect, an unveiled spiritual perception, a brotherliness for all, a readiness to give and receive advice and instruction, a loyal sense of duty to the Teacher, a willing obedience to the behests of Truth, a courageous endurance of personal injustice, a brave declaration of principles, a valiant defence of those who are unjustly attacked, and a constant eye to the ideal of human progression and perfection which the Sacred Science depicts. These are the Golden Stairs up the steps of which the learner may climb to the Temple of Divine Wisdom.

The gateway leads inward only, and closes behind the neophyte for evermore.

That hidden or occult science of life is in the keeping of the Adept Brotherhood, and is imparted by degrees to the disciple who proves worthy of the trust. But quite apart from this a man may mount to the higher realms of consciousness, and to this end all systems of Yoga are adapted.

CHAPTER XXV

PRAYER AND MEDITATION

DOES a Theosophist "believe in" prayer? Do they prefer to "meditate"? These are the kind of questions often asked. Prayer is good wherever offered and of whatever kind. The primitive, ignorant man may, like a little child, look upon the Eternal Life as a very personal being like himself, and as one from whom he may ask personal favours. And who shall say where and how the compassionate Heart of the Universe answers such prayers?

But the prayer of a Saint or a Sage has long passed beyond personal requests. It takes on the quality of adoration, absorption into the Infinite Beauty. All prayer, from its most primitive, childish form to the high-vaulted soaring of the illumined soul is an attempt to approach the Heart of Being, to become more and more "in tune with the Infinite". And surely as man approaches Deity, even more surely does Deity stoop to him. There never was a prayer of any kind that found not its answer somewhere, somehow.

We could define prayer in many ways. A Quaker author calls it a "love-relation between God and the Soul". Gerald Massey defines it as the "inexpressible longing of the inner man for the Infinite". Another definition similar to this last is that it is "a sigh lying upon the human heart". Whatever it is, it is always an effort to elevate the soul to the Infinite, and he who makes a habit of prayer is more likely to live in peace and inspiration than he who never casts his thoughts heavenwards. There is a beautiful little book written by the famous Dr. Alexis Carrell on "Prayer", and in it he says:

> It is by prayer that man reaches to God and that God enters into him. Man needs God as he needs water and oxygen.

The man whose whole attention is centred upon things visible becomes narrowed, restless, uninspired; his hungry soul becomes mute and faint. "Now faith is the substance of things hoped for, the evidence of things, not seen. . . . For the things which are seen are temporal; but the things which are not seen are eternal." At least once a day let a man turn his thoughts to eternal things and the best time is in the early morning, so that they will sing in his heart all through the ensuing day.

Are we approaching the subject of meditation? Meditation is a kind of prayer. Sometimes it reaches a height when words and even defined ideas cease, and the soul is held in beatitude, gazing into Infinity and being blessed thereby. But such heights may be too far for most of us. Yet even the lower reaches are productive of great good.

The results of prayer and meditation should not be judged by personal feelings of happiness or satisfaction, lovely as these may be. All sorts of circumstances, some of them physical, may be accountable for seeming dryness of response. Annie Besant once wrote: "There is no relation between our progress and our feelings. There are tides in the human heart as in the affairs of men." To be restless and dissatisfied is equivalent to "bargaining with Eternity", and this can never be done. Nor are visions and supernatural happenings necessarily any evidence of advance in prayer. Results are more truly shown in the gradual deepening and purifying of the character, the widening of the mental outlook, the ever more sensitive response to the needs of others and to the beauty around us.

Will you tell us how to meditate? so many people ask. The path of meditation is the path inwards of the soul to Eternity, and is a very individual path, unique to the man himself. He *is* the Path. Yet something can be said. The easiest way is to begin with some lovely thought. Sit up in bed in the morning for five or even ten minutes, and read some beautiful lines embodying a deep truth, from a scripture, if you will. Close the eyes in order to shut out the sights and sounds of earth, and dwell in thought upon the lines, trying to see its meaning and implications, and waiting in peace for "Lights" or inspirations to shine in. Do not trouble if you cannot shut out sounds. In time you will not hear them.

Another form of meditation is to picture a Divine Ideal, say the Lord Christ, or some other great Son of God, and to let our heart flow out in love and gratitude towards Him. The love and inward contemplation of a Divine Ideal has a very potent and ennobling effect upon the character. Never mind if no love force stirs in us. One day it will, for "we needs must love the Highest when we see it". What we think upon we finally become. To love and adore something is to grow like it. Thus to King Arthur, through the adoring company of his knights, flashed "the image of the King".

Let us find our own way, aspire, yearn after God if haply we may find Him. And those moments of inward elevation should always be closed with the thought of others. We are at our strongest to help them. Bring them into the Light too in thought. Pray blessing and help for them and leave them in thought in "the Everlasting Arms".

Sometimes we can think over the duties of the day and how best we may accomplish them, for prayer and meditation are not only a way of asking, but a way of *being taught*.

It is the habitual turning of the soul to God that helps. Five minutes a day is more valuable than an hour once a week, and who is there who cannot give five minutes every day?

Do not necessarily drop into an orthodox religious attitude about this. The spiritual life and spiritual aspirations are the most "natural", healthy, properly normal things in the world. We all yearn for the Infinite. Let that express itself in the way most natural and beautiful to each. Some of the great poets are as inspired by Life as the scriptures. Nature herself has a wonderful voice, if we can listen to her. To the man whose inner eyes are opened:

> Earth's crammed with heaven,
> And every common bush afire with God
> But only he who sees, takes off his shoes.
>
> E. B. Browning

A wonderful description of this kind of meditation will be found in Wordsworth's poems. He describes:

> That blessed mood,
> In which the burthen of the mystery,
> In which the heavy and the weary weight
> Of all this unintelligible world
> Is lightened—that serene and blessed mood
> In which the affections gently lead us on
> Until, the breath of this corporeal frame,
> And even the motion of our human blood,
> Almost suspended, we are laid asleep
> In body, and become a living soul.

Long years ago I tried to find what to me was "God". It was not Righteousness, which could be so cold and hard; not Truth, so austere and implacable; not even Love, as men understood it in their selfish way. Then I saw it was Beauty. Ah! what is the Beautiful, so fine, so delicate, so exquisite a thing? The Beautiful is too fine and sensitive a thing to be cruel, or hard, or unloving. Where there is Beauty there is joy, love, peace, selflessness. Thus my God became the Beautiful and so He remains to this day.

One of the most beautiful meditations in the world was described by the Lord Buddha when one day an aspiring monk came to Him, to ask Him to show him the way to the Land of Eternal Happiness. " In truth ", the Lord replied, " there is such a paradise, but it is a spiritual country, and accessible only to those who are spiritual."

" Teach me, Lord," answered the monk, " the meditations to which I must devote myself in order to let my mind enter into this paradise."

The Lord said: " There are four great meditations. The first is the meditation of love, in which you must so adjust your heart that you long for the weal and welfare of all beings, including the happiness of your enemies.

" The second meditation is the meditation of pity, in which you think of all beings in distress, vividly representing in your imagination their sorrows and anxieties so as to arouse a deep compassion for them in your soul.

" The third meditation is the meditation of joy, in which you think of the prosperity of others and rejoice with their rejoicings.

" The fourth is the meditation of serenity, in which you rise above love and hate, tyranny and oppression, wealth and want, and regard your own fate with impartial calmness and perfect tranquillity."

CHAPTER XXVI

WORLD EVENTS IN THE LIGHT OF OCCULTISM

Dr. Annie Besant once said that all would-be occultists should read the daily papers with the thought of the great Plan in their minds, trying to detect, if they could, the hand of the great Adepts in world affairs. For there is a heavenly Plan for all life on this planet, and to glimpse it is to gain a feeling of security and hope.

In the archives of the Adept Brotherhood are kept records of the past history of man on this planet, outdating anything known to history as we know it. Our history goes back a few thousand years, though it is true that geology tells us more of pre-historic man. Civilizations rise and fall like the waves of the sea, but behind them all is the steady pressure of evolutionary intent. Thousands and thousands of years ago there were civilizations and populations as great as any we have now. For instance, the fabulous Atlanteans, now recognized as having truly existed, employed air-ships, (though they were not driven by the same power as we employ). These civilizations have disappeared, and with them their culture and knowledge. However, mankind is now reaching a point where this may not happen again.

If we telescope enormous periods of time in thought we can state that, during the life-time of this planet, seven major types or races of men, called Root Races, will be evolved, each one an advance upon the previous ones both in appearance and in the subtlety and co-ordination of the nervous system. The slow development takes place gradually but surely, with many accompanying apparent set-backs and withdrawals, occupying what may well run into millions of years. For instance, the leading race today is the Aryan race, although it is not yet numerically the largest. It is the Fifth Root Race of the series, and it began to appear over a million years ago. Two more are still to come, but do not let us imagine that the " end of the world " is near. Vast periods still remain.

Where are the former Root Races and their records? The first two we will not discuss for they were scarcely human as we understand it, and lived in more etherial bodies than ours when the climate of the earth was far hotter. The first densely physical human men were the members of the Third Root Race, and they lived millions of years ago on this earth. The Root Races can be characterized, as ethnologists still classify man, by the shape of the head, the texture of the hair, and the colour of the skin.

The Third Root Race men were ebony black in colour, with round-shaped skulls and crinkly hair. Their descendants, no longer pure in descent, are to be seen in all the negroid peoples of the earth today. But the earliest were also much bigger men than are to be seen today, sometimes reaching as much as 20 feet in height. " Giants dwelt therein in old time."

Every great Root Race inevitably splits into permutations and off-shoots, or sub-races, and these in turn form families of nations. Slowly, from the old sub-races the new Root Race begins to emerge after slow approximations thereto.

The Fourth Root Race was the famed Atlantean race. Anyone who doubts that Atlantis really existed should read Ignatius Donnelly's *Atlantis,* for he has there marshalled the evidence, such as the same flora and fauna, the similar architectural remains, on both sides of the Atlantic, in a very convincing fashion. We should here note that over these vast periods of time the configuration of the land alters. It seems to be a necessity that the earth must spend a certain time beneath the waters of the sea to become thoroughly iodinized. Whether this be true or not, the land surface of the globe is always slowly but surely shifting. In the British Isles certain parts are being encroached on by the sea, others building up. By volcanic agency islands appear and disappear. In the Himālaya Mountains, the highest in the world, fossil remains of sea-animals and shells are found, showing that they were once under the sea. The islands of the Azores are the peaks of mighty mountains four miles in depth under the sea. The ancient records say that the land alters alternately by fire and water, i.e. by volcanic agency and the creation of huge tidal waves, the latter seems to have given rise to the universal tradition of a " Flood " among all nations.

To return to the Atlanteans, they were a people of long heads, straight hair, and red-brown or yellowish skins, with high cheek-bones and slightly oblique eyes. Their descendants are easily distinguishable in the vast populations of the Mongolian peoples of today. It was mentioned that there was also a difference in the complexity and sensitivity of the nervous system, though *all* races today tend to approximate in this particular to the Aryan man. The last remnant of ancient Atlantis is mentioned by Plato, as lying beyond the " Pillars of Hercules ", the Straits of Gibraltar.

The Fifth Root Race, the Aryan, began to appear as stated, about a million years ago, and its permutation into sub-races is not yet complete. At present there are three main ethnic groups, the colder, more intellectual (on the whole) Teutonic peoples, including the German, Dutch, Scandinavian and English peoples; the warmer, more emotional and artistic Latin peoples, comprising the races of Southern Europe, such as the Spanish, French, Italian, Greek, and including also certain elements among the Irish and Highland Scotch; lastly, the mysterious Slav race, comprising the Russians and peoples of Eastern Europe, Arabia and Egypt, India and Persia.

One other fact: language shows an advance with each Root Race. The language of the Lemurians, the Third Root Race, largely consisted of imitative and descriptive terms for natural objects around. Their vocabulary was small, as is the speech of some primitive peoples today. The speech of the Atlanteans was enlarged by the putting together of words, called by ethnologists "agglutinative", with few particles or inflexions. This can be seen today in the language of the little pockets of their descendants in Europe, such as the Finns, Hungarians and Basques. It remained for the Aryan Race to develop inflectional speech.

Is the Sixth Root Race already appearing? Hardly. That will not really occur for some hundreds of years yet, but its gradual approximations are appearing in all the "new" countries, such as America, Australasia and South Africa. There are certain slight exterior signs but a noticeable one is an increased psychic sensitivity joined to a natural generosity of spirit. The more "advanced" souls are coming into incarnation now, and it is they who will lead the race to greater heights. But sometimes they suffer for being born a little ahead of others. The coming into being of this more sensitive and generous-minded race is one of the reasons for the mighty and cataclysmic changes taking place in the world today, in all spheres of man's being, religious, political, sociological, artistic.

Perhaps we shall understand this better if we remember that Life proceeds by great cycles, or ages following each other like the waves of the sea, or like the chain of day following day. Astrologers are acquainted with this principle. They will tell us of cycles of time following each other by the Sun moving into another sign of the Zodiac. We are now leaving the Piscean Age (the Age of the Fishes which governed the Christian Era) and passing into the Age of Aquarius, the era of universality, typified by the symbol of the Water-bearer, a man pouring water from a jar. It will be indeed the Age of Unity when war and poverty cease for the rest of the life of this planet, and " the earth shall be full of the knowledge of the Lord, as the waters cover the sea ". For the Sixth Root Race will be a spiritually minded race, and human institutions and civilizations must be framed accordingly. That is the meaning of the gigantic interplay of forces in the world today. A new age is being hammered out on the anvil of time—hastened by the agony of the World War. It was one World war, not two, with an uneasy interlude in between, and there will never be another. By that crucifixion of the world, by that tremendous hastening of universal karma, changes are now possible which would otherwise have taken hundreds of years to accomplish. It is almost as if mankind having been too blind, ignorant and selfish to see the things which belonged unto its peace, they were now hid from its eyes and the flail of God descended.

The doctrine of great ages or Yugas was known both to India and Greece. H. P. Blavatsky before her death stated that the Kali Yuga, " black " or Iron Age, began in 3,102 B.C., that we have recently come to the close of its first five thousand years, and that " the great European nations have now reached their iron age—an age *black with horrors*. They are moving onward through ways unmarked from guilt to punishment." What a true description of the present day?

But the end of a cycle means two things, the break-up of the old order of things and the coming in of the new. "The old order changeth, yielding place to new, and God fulfils Himself in many ways." Like the onward waves of the tide the ages, great and small, pass. If we are dim and narrow of vision we shall only see the wave which is breaking on the shores of Time, and hence universal disintegration; but if we have vision (without which "the people perish") we shall discern the wave which is coming on behind, on the crest of which, to use Annie Besant's splendid simile, rides the Spirit of the Future. To that let us raise our eyes today, for even today we can discern the first, faint shadowings of the dawn, the first faint fingers shooting up into the sky which presages a Day that will dawn, happier and better by far than any humanity has yet known. For we stand at the parting of the ways, at the most tremendous moment that has ever yet struck this globe. All things, all forms, material or immaterial, all systems, methods, institutions, are in the melting-pot, and the great question in this for all is, are they elastic enough to be adapted to the rising tide of Life? If not, they must break, and be cast aside for, as the Christian Teacher told us, new wine cannot be put into old bottles. Let us try to trace this happening in every department of human life, and this resolves itself mainly into two divisions, the inner and the outer side of life, the one dependent upon the other, namely the religious world or the world of man's soul and Spirit, and the outer world, the spheres of political and social activity and change.

In the religious world a most remarkable change is to be observed. It has been dwelt upon elsewhere in this book. As before stated, the world is passing from the contemplation of God Transcendent to God Immanent, and most of all in the depths of the human soul. Hence the extraordinary and ever-mounting interest in the things of the Spirit, and with the lives and sayings of those of all ages who were pre-eminently holy, " God-intoxicated " men and women. No longer is humanity interested in dogma and theology, but in first-hand religious experience. Gone are the days when mysticism was regarded as " an exploded superstition ". I think the turn of the tide was much helped by the assertions of the venerable Dean Inge, in his notable books on the subject of mysticism, that it was the only real, valid form of religion, and that without its great mystics every great religion would soon die. " We want a new reformation," he wrote, " it will be neither fundamentalist nor modernist; but it will rest upon mysticism, which is the practice of the Presence of God, and upon rationalism, which means confidence in Science." A " new religion " is coming into the world, a universal religion, suited to the growing sense of the unity of all mankind, more valid because more *real*, a religion founded upon an increasing knowledge of God, not upon dogmatic utterances and theological rulings, which are after all but symbols indicating a supernal truth. A dogma is a materialized symbol which by that very materialization through the passage of years and the spiritual ignorance of man, has largely lost its supreme value, and instead of indicating a way has now become a prison-house to the mind and Spirit of the ordinary man. Life ever goes on. Life ever increases, and finds for itself a freer and a nobler embodiment than the out-worn shell it is quitting. Says Oliver Wendell Homes:

> Build thee more stately mansions, O my soul,
> As the swift seasons roll!
> Leave thy low-vaulted past!
> Let each new temple, nobler than the last,
> Shut thee from heaven with a dome more vast,
> Till thou at length art free,
> Leaving thine outgrown shell by life's unresting sea!

Two other forces are also to be noted in the interior world of man's soul: one is the growing touch with the world invisible, and the other is the passing of emphasis from the thought of our Lord the Christ's death to the thought of His ever-living Presence among us. It is not His death at the hands of ignorant men, but His ever-living Presence amongst us, who said, " Lo, I am with you alway, even unto the end of the world," which saves men.

Now, there cannot be an advance towards the sense of Unity within, without a corresponding growth of the sense of Brotherhood without. In spite of wars, old hatreds and universal fear and uncertainty, that perception and feeling are steadily growing. This is what all men desire in their inmost hearts—to live at peace, to be friends. Can it come? It is coming, and in a few hundred years it will rule life and bring about the end of the greatest evils that afflict mankind, war and poverty, which are two sides of the same coin.

To envisage the social tendencies of this world correctly, let us take as a guide the great Italian thinker and patriot, Joseph Mazzini. Although he lived so many years ago, and apparently knew nothing of Occultism, yet he had clearly formulated in his own mind, the occult doctrine of cycles, and detected the "message" of each succeeding one. His theory is that every age formulates a great over-shadowing thought, which is only verified in the sphere of action when the advancing human intellect is already absorbed in the contemplation of the thought of its successor. Thus he says:

> The *thesis* of the Middle Ages is the *principle* of the present day; the idea of the Middle Ages is now a recognized, admitted law. Does anyone now deny liberty and equality in *principle*? The most illiberal ruler asserts that he is the protector of the rights and liberties of his subjects against the anarchy of factions. The question is, in the sphere of principles, decided. The only struggle is as to its application. The dispute no longer regards the law itself, but its interpretations.

Then he goes on to say:

> The first epoch of Christianity was to constitute *individual man* as he was destined to be—free, sacred, inviolable. And this mission was accomplished

through the French Revolution, which was the political translation of the Protestant Revolution. . . . The declaration of the *rights of man* is the supreme and ultimate formula of the French Revolution. . . . Ruins there were without end; but in the midst of these ruins and negations, one immense affirmation stood erect; the creature of God, ready to act, radiant in power and will; *Ecce Homo*, repeated after eighteen centuries of struggle and suffering; not by the voice of the martyr, but from the altar raised by the Revolution to victory—right, the faith of individuality, rooted in the world for ever.

But to Mazzini the rule of the free and equal citizen must be tempered by love, not by the ambitions of power-drunk men. He writes wonderful words about love:

Love! Love is the flight of the soul towards God, towards the Great, the Sublime and the Beautiful, which are the shadows of God upon earth. Love your family, the partner of your life, those around you ready to share your joys and sorrows, the dead who were dear to you and to whom you were dear. But let your love be the love taught to you by Dante; the love of souls that aspire together, and do not grovel on the earth in search of a felicity which it is not the destiny of the creature here to reach; do not yield to a delusion which inevitably would degrade you into egotism. To love is to promise and to receive a promise for the future. God has given us love that the weary soul may give and receive support upon the path of life. It is a flower which springs upon the path of duty, but which cannot change its course.

This love must come into all human relationships. Tolstoy once wrote of the kind of business, called

Government Service, which allows men to treat other men as things, without any brotherly relations with them. "It all lives in the fact," writes he, "that men think there are circumstances when one may deal with human beings without love. But there are no such circumstances, for material love is the fundamental law of human life. . . . If you feel no love, sit still, occupy yourself with things, only not with man."

Mazzini said that the keynote of this closing age was the recognition of the "rights of man". This was never possible before, for all past ages and civilizations were founded upon a vast substructure of slavery and serfdom, of millions who had no rights and were the personal property of their owners. Egypt, Rome, Chaldea, and even the gracious life of Greece, were all upheld by this army of the voiceless, the unknown. The slave population of Greece far outnumbered their owners.

It remained for this era to destroy slavery for evermore, at least in principle. The conscience of modern man will not tolerate the idea that men can hold the bodies of other men as their personal possession. It may be argued that "wage-slavery" still exists. True, but the idea is firmly established in the consciousness of men, and it will expand there. Presently it will be seen that it is just as immoral to own and control the primal necessities of all men's living as it is to own their bodies. It paid the old slave-owner to feed and treat his slaves well, as one feeds a valuable animal. But who minds about the conditions of the "wage-slave", thrown out by a diminishing market? But that too is passing. The conscience of mankind is a kind of common denominator. The best people are ahead of it, the worst people behind. But over the mass it slowly rises. Look back even a hundred years and note its slow rise. A hundred years ago the public conscience tolerated public hangings and floggings, the working of little children in the mines and factories, the horrors of the convict ships, and the savage sentences imposed for the mildest of offences. These things no longer exist.

It is true, even if we cite the awful rise of juvenile crime and of criminal offences everywhere after the war. War always brings these things. The old landmarks have been removed and the new ones are not yet clearly seen. Furthermore, the basis of much crime is poverty and inequality of opportunity. This, too, is slowly passing.

I said that the World War hastened this process. In spite of its horrors, that is true. Sometimes the forces of Nature do not wait for man's slow comprehension, and moving swiftly, produce temporary disaster. A factor of cataclysmic change occurred during the Victorian era, the coming of machinery. Up to that moment England possessed a large rural population. Until the destruction of the monasteries by Henry VIII, the unlettered poor were cared for in sickness and old age by the monks. Under Elizabeth I, the vagrant population of England had attained such dimensions that very harsh laws were enacted against them. Yet in the reign of Edward III, when England was called "Merrie England" the French Ambassador wrote to his Sovereign of the happiness and health of the rural population.

At the coming of machinery the rural population streamed into the towns, and England passed from being an agricultural people to an industrial one. Until the outbreak of the World War large tracts of arable land in England remained uncultivated, or became parks and hunting-grounds for a privileged nobility. The "common lands", whereon the peasantry used to graze their cattle, were enclosed by selfish landlords.

Nevertheless, agriculture remains the backbone of every country. One of the wisest men who ever lived, the great Benjamin Franklin, said this. He writes:

> There seems to be but three ways for a nation to acquire wealth. The first is by war, as the Romans did, in plundering their conquered neighbours. This is robbery. The second is by commerce, which is generally cheating. The third is by agriculture, the only honest way, wherein man received a real increase of the seed thrown into the ground, in a kind of continual miracle wrought by the hand of God in his favour, as a reward for his innocent life and his virtuous industry.

The horrors of the first years of the industrial age do not need repeating. They can all be found recorded in the life of the great and good Lord Shaftesbury. One little scene always remains in my mind. A compassionate overseer was conducting Lord Shaftesbury over a cotton mill. In those days little children, sometimes of six or seven, were employed to stand long hours beside the weavers, handing them the threads. They approached one little girl of six. "Look!" said the overseer. The child was dead asleep on her feet, but still, in her sleep, mechanically handled the threads. Boys and girls were used to draw the trucks of coal that ponies drag now.

No wonder that the old-time weavers looked upon the new machines as their enemy and tried to break them! From one point of view they were right. But the clock of time cannot be put back. Every day new improvements in machinery throw more men out of work. What once took dozens of men to accomplish can now be done by one. What is the answer? The answer is clear to all who will see.

In a properly arranged, fully co-operative world—and this can never come about as long as classes and nations selfishly fight for their own interests and advantages, their own "sovereign rights"—the hours of labour all over the world will be gradually reduced. In the end no one will work more than four hours a day, nor will any child be in school for longer. "What!" many people will exclaim, "what shall we do with so much leisure?" They will probably quote the old adage about Satan finding some mischief still for idle hands to do.

But we shall learn to employ our leisure. We shall learn to live and to be. Millions of people today do not live, they merely exist. They rush to a dingy office all day, enjoying sunshine only perhaps on Sundays; they work long hours at a deadly monotonous job until the soul of them becomes a machine too. In ancient times an artisan could be an artist at his trade and take a pride in it. Today he tends a soulless machine and makes a bit of a thing. "We have no time," wrote the Welsh poet, W. H. Davies, "to stand and stare." No time to think, to dream, to love beauty, to get into touch with Nature.

"How Utopian?" many will say, "and utterly impossible!" But it will surely come. In the words of Gerald Heard, scientist and mystic: "A new Age of leisure is in sight—but many currents can keep mankind from ever reaching that shore." But they will reach it, because the Gods have so ordained. The future synthesis of the coming age is dawning now. Mazzini saw it and put it into words. "The synthesis of the coming age is Collective Humanity, and we are bound to organize the family and the nation towards that supreme Ideal."

All the forces of Life are leading up to it. What have electricity, steamships, newspapers, the wireless, done for us? They have bound the whole world into one, are making us increasingly "world-conscious". Two thousand years ago half the world did not know the other half existed; intercommunication was very slow. Today, that which happens in the most remote quarters of the globe is known in a few hours to all the world. In a few hours one can fly to any quarter of the globe. Man will be a citizen of the world, and Tennyson's dream of "the Parliament of man, the Federation of the world" will come true.

I cannot forbear to quote here the words of India's noble poet, Rabindranath Tagore:

> Where the mind is without fear
> And the head is held high;
> Where knowledge is free;
> Where the world has not been broken into fragments of narrow domestic walls;
> Into that heaven of freedom, my Father, let my country awake.

I said the World War had hastened it—in this way among others. Before the onset of the great World War there was such stress and strain between classes, capital and labour, that we wondered whether there were any way out besides "bloody revolution". The war showed the way out. In face of a common danger, imperilling the whole nation, class-struggle agreed to cease for the time being. The principle is clear. The keynote of the coming age is "Collective Humanity", and its consequent principle of action is "Co-operation". The violent assertions of the preceding age had led up to this, for co-operation is only possible between strongly established self-hoods conscious of their dignity and rights. It is not possible to a slave mentality. The principle of co-operation is easily to be seen, if one tries to walk down a crowded street determined not to give way to the right or the left! Co-operation means that each side is willing to give way a little in pursuance of a further ideal which includes them both. In face of a common danger this was done during the war, and a wonderfully united spirit supervened.

Now that same principle must be applied between nations on a world-wide scale. Each nation's rights and dignity must be respected—"empires" and the colonial system are passing; and each nation must learn to forgo its "sovereign rights" for the sake of the peace and happiness of all humanity. This will also extend itself to the economic world. What a different world it will be when we no longer fight to grab markets and exploit primitive peoples, but by world-wide planning bring the peculiar produce of each nation to those quarters of the globe where it is most needed. Perhaps one day freight carriage and human travel will be world-wide and free that we may all grow to *know* and therefore to appreciate one another!

I have every sympathy with what is called the Revolt of Asia. The World War destroyed for ever the superiority of the West in the mind of the East. The civilizations of India and China are far older than ours. The West can help them, in the technological side of life, with roads, engineering, sanitation, freedom from stale customs and age-old superstition. But the East can also help the West with their immemorial patience and faith in life, and their magnificent ancient scriptures. It is a fair exchange.

One hope of the world is the British Commonwealth of Free Nations. It is no longer an Empire. Empires are out of date. It is a model for all the world to copy, and join it in time, of a community of free nations, held together by no other bond than mutual respect and friendship. I think the world government will be led up to at first by the forming of mighty federations of nations, foremost amongst which is the coming United States of Europe.

The great Napoleon, power-drunk as he may have been, had that idea in mind, but he went the wrong way about to achieve it. In his memoirs written in St. Helena, this passage occurs:

> In my way Europe might soon have become a single nation, and any man wherever he travelled might have felt he was in his native country all the time. This amalgamation will come sooner or later by the force of circumstances; the impulse is there, and I believe that after my fall and the disappearance of my system no lasting equilibrium will be possible except through the amalgamation and confederation of the great nations.

Mutual co-operation is the real heart of democracy. True democracy is not yet achieved, and this is partly due to the reign of the Party System, laying things open to rule by a caucus or by selfish vested interests. The men who form the final Council of a Nation should already have proved their worth, integrity and ability, in smaller fields of service, such as provincial and city governments, quite independently of any party or organized group after power.

A Master of the Wisdom, long years ago, told Annie Besant what the rise of the idea of democracy really meant. He said that the vast mass of men, whom we designate the proletariat, and who had in the past been mostly slaves, were now reaching a point where their spiritual unfoldment could begin, but that this was held up and frustrated by the tremendous inequality and uncertainty of life. Therefore, He said, it had been decreed that this inequality and uncertainty must begin to leave the world. Does this not explain why nearly every country is now talking about social security?

Does this imply that Socialism or Communism is bound to come everywhere? I hold no brief for any 'ism, only for the innate kindliness of the human heart set free of fear and greed, and its native common sense. But the writing on the wall is clear. Let us put it this way: some form of co-operative living, both within the nation, and between the nations, is bound to come. May it come happily, generously, and not at the price of human bloodshed.

The dawning age will see the end of both war and poverty. But what about the atomic bomb, some will ask, are we not on the brink of a still more awful world war? Here I will quote the words of another great Adept, again to Annie Besant, spoken many years ago when Sir Oliver Lodge was discoursing upon the possibility of science unlocking the illimitable power contained in the atom, and which will give us, Sir Oliver said, light, heat and motive power in the future. "We will not allow that to be discovered," the Master said, "until the threat of war has passed."

Had the threat of war passed when that was done in 1945? Not to our eyes, but it may be to the longer, deeper vision of the Adept. I feel sure that there will never be another world war upon this planet. I also feel that before so very long we shall also get into communication with other man-bearing planets.

How fortunate are we who can know these truths. We may well echo the noble words of Pythagoras: "Take courage; the race of men is divine." Slowly but surely humanity is rising out of the shadow into the shine. Always there are its great and perfected Elder Brothers to help it mount. H. P. B. said that at the close of every century the Great Brotherhood made a special effort to help and enlighten mankind. At the close of the last century, They sponsored the birth of the Theosophical Society, bringing to men the barest outline of the sacred science, and becoming the parent of numerous other movements all veering in the same direction.

The close of the present century is not far off. A "new torch-bearer of Truth" will come; and many believe and hope that it will be the Spiritual Head of the world, in whose care are all the souls of men, whether inside or outside the organized forms of religion.

Two thousand years ago His disciples asked the World Teacher what would be the signs of His coming again and the end of the world? If we may put it thus: "What shall be the signs of Thy reappearance and the end of the age?" How typical of the present hour was the Lord's reply that there would be wars and rumours of wars, famines, and pestilences, and earthquakes, and men's hearts failing them for fear. But they are the marks of the old order passing and the coming of the new.

"Amen, come, Lord."

CHAPTER XXVII

FAREWELL

THIS book of mine is finished. I have tried to put in it what I have learnt and felt concerning the common life around us and its meaning; and also of the instruments of that lovely and supernal growth—body, soul, and Spirit. In another book I will try to trace the method of growth of man's soaring Spirit towards the love and bliss which ever live at the heart of life.

So many who read these lines may have listened to me and heard me in the past. And so many, even those whose names I have forgotten, I remember still and can never forget. Some I have only seen once, as ships that pass in the night, yet they are still with me in consciousness as vividly as when I met them.

God be with you, my many friends, until we meet again. In the world of the Spirit we never part, though down here it seems like a temporary farewell!

CHAPTER XXVII

FAREWELL

This book of mine is finished. I have tried to put in it what I have learnt and felt concerning the common life around us and its meaning, and also of the instruments of that lovely and supernal growth—body, soul, and spirit. In another book I will try to trace the method of growth of man's soaring Spirit towards the love and bliss which ever live at the heart of life.

So many who read these lines may have listened to me and heard me in the past. And so many, even those whose names I have forgotten, I remember still and can never forget. Some I have only seen once; as ships that pass in the night, yet they are still with me in consciousness as vividly as when I met them.

God be with you, my many friends, until we meet again. In the world of the Spirit we never part, though down here it seems like a temporary farewell!